Routines
for Reasoning

Grace Kelemanik • Amy Lucenta • Susan Janssen Creighton

FOREWORD BY Magdalene Lampert

Routines
for Reasoning

Fostering the
Mathematical
Practices in
All Students

HEINEMANN
Portsmouth, NH

Heinemann
361 Hanover Street
Portsmouth, NH 03801–3912
www.heinemann.com

Offices and agents throughout the world

> *The authors have dedicated a great deal of time and effort to writing the content of this book, and their written expression is protected by copyright law. We respectfully ask that you do not adapt, reuse, or copy anything on third-party (whether for-profit or not-for-profit) lesson-sharing websites. As always, we're happy to answer any questions you may have.*
> **—Heinemann Publishers**

The authors and publisher wish to thank those who have generously given permission to reprint borrowed material:

Excerpts from the Common Core State Standards © Copyright 2010. National Governors Association Center for Best Practices and Council of Chief State School Officers. All rights reserved.

The Massachusetts Comprehensive Assessment System (MCAS) sample materials are included by permission of the Massachusetts Department of Elementary and Secondary Education. Inclusion does not constitute endorsement of any commercial publication.

Acknowledgments for borrowed material continue on page 189.

Library of Congress Cataloging-in-Publication Data
Names: Kelemanik, Grace. | Lucenta, Amy. | Creighton, Susan Janssen.
Title: Routines for reasoning : fostering the mathematical practices in all
    students / Grace Kelemanik, Amy Lucenta, Susan Janssen Creighton.
Description: Portsmouth, NH : Heinemann, [2016] | Includes bibliographical
    references.
Identifiers: LCCN 2016029349 | ISBN 9780325078151
Subjects: LCSH: Mathematics—Study and teaching—Standards—United States.
Classification: LCC QA13 .K45 2016 | DDC 510.71/073—dc23
LC record available at https://lccn.loc.gov/2016029349

Editor: Katherine Bryant
Production: Vicki Kasabian
Interior and cover designs: Suzanne Heiser
Cover photograph: © Yagi Studios/Getty Images
Typesetter: Shawn Girsberger
Manufacturing: Steve Bernier

Printed in the United States of America on acid-free paper
20 19   VP   4 5

For Mark Driscoll,
whose unwavering respect for teachers
and fierce commitment to success for every student
serve as a beacon for all.

Contents

1 Using the Math Practices as a Means to Provide Access to Rich Mathematical Reasoning   1

2 Instructional Routines: A Vehicle for Developing Mathematical Practices in All Students   18

3 Capturing Quantities: An Instructional Routine to Support Students Reasoning Abstractly and Quantitatively   41

4 Connecting Representations: An Instructional Routine to Support Students Thinking About and with Mathematical Structure   73

Foreword

In 1989, the National Council of Teachers of Mathematics issued *Curriculum and Evaluation Standards for School Mathematics*, proposing not only rigorous mathematical content standards but the idea that the school curriculum should involve students at all levels in *doing mathematics*. They called for more cooperative work, discussion, questioning, justification of thinking, and content integration. In 1991, in the *Professional Standards for Teaching Mathematics*, NCTM called on teachers to pose questions and tasks that would elicit, engage, and challenge each student's thinking, to listen carefully to students' ideas, and to ask students to clarify and justify their ideas orally and in writing. In 1999, however, the TIMMS Videotape Classroom Study reported that American teachers and students at the eighth-grade level continued to spend 90 percent of their time in mathematics classes practicing routine procedures. The Common Core State Standards (CCSS), launched in 2009, reiterated the importance of students engaging in mathematical practices, both to learn the practices themselves and to learn grade-level-appropriate content.

From my own investigations of the work of teaching authentic mathematics to all students, I knew that the kinds of things that NCTM and CCSS were asking teachers to do were fundamentally different from what is required for teaching routine procedures. Asking students to clarify and justify their ideas, for example, would involve a cultural shift in how classroom interaction was organized. Most important, teaching mathematical practices would need to be supported by a whole new technology of instruction. We know the routines for demonstration and practicing procedures. Most of us were taught mathematics that way. But what could we put in place of these common routines that would *actually engage students in doing mathematics*?

From the teacher's point of view this is a very practical question. In a lesson organized around work like finding and using structure, reasoning abstractly and quantitatively, or

making sense and persevering in problem solving, what are the teacher and the students to do first, next, and next? How should they be seated in the room? What should be written on the board when, and by whom? Who talks to whom when, and about what? Exactly how does one elicit, engage, and challenge each student's thinking? What can a teacher do in any part of a lesson to get students to clarify and justify their ideas? And how is doing these mathematical practices related to teaching and learning content according to a given scope and sequence?

From my own investigation of authentic mathematics teaching, I knew that it was possible to do such teaching and learning. I also knew that using well-designed classroom routines every day could disrupt common notions that teaching math was only about telling and guiding students' work on procedural exercises. But it would not be a simple matter of issuing new standards or changing assessments.

Mathematical reasoning requires students to be attentive to both the content and to one another. Listening to students' ideas and building from them to a rigorous mathematical curriculum requires extraordinary concentration on the part of the teacher. New instructional routines were needed to make it possible to manage thirty students in one room while they were reasoning and critiquing the reasoning of others, as well as to make it possible for students to construct new kinds of relationships with their classmates, in which it would be safe to say what they think and appropriate to raise questions about someone else's thinking. Instructional routines could enable both students and teacher to focus on the mathematics rather than on who is supposed to be doing what when. And they could change what we think it means to learn in math class.

How could these routines be designed, compiled, and named in ways that might make the simultaneous "doing" of mathematics, teaching, and learning clear? How could they be positioned in relation to all of the different kinds of mathematics content that students are expected to learn?

In my search for answers to these questions, I found my way to a teacher education program in Rome for teachers of Italian that organized ambitious language teaching and learning around a small set of regularly enacted Instructional Activities. These IAs were to be used by teachers routinely to engage learners at all levels in solving authentic problems of reading, writing, speaking, and listening in a new language. They are designed precisely to enable teachers to teach by eliciting, interpreting, and responding to students' efforts to make sense of language and use it to communicate.

I also found my way to balanced literacy, a comprehensive approach that makes use of a set of instructional components, or routines (such as reading and writing workshop, shared reading, interactive writing, word study, and read-aloud) for organizing the teaching and learning of literacy. In both designs for instruction, routines allow for numerous variations in content while preserving consistent structures. These models made me hopeful that such a design could bring mathematics teaching and learning in school closer to the real work of doing mathematics. In 2005, my colleagues at the University of Washington, UCLA, and the University of Michigan and I began to work on this idea in the Learning Teaching Practice Project with a focus on elementary mathematics.

In 2010, I met Grace Kelemanik, who became my colleague in bringing performance-oriented professional education to the Boston Teacher Residency. Grace had her own set of ideas about using routines to organize teaching and learning so that novice teachers would be able to do the demanding work of developing mathematical practices in all students. With Amy Lucenta and Susan Creighton, Grace has worked with numerous teachers from all kinds of classrooms to hone a set of mathematical thinking routines to be used in schools. These routines are practical tools for teachers. They are designed around a predictable set of actions that students and teachers can learn and then do repeatedly until they fall into the background—so that the challenging work of doing mathematics can come to the foreground. Using the routines described in this book can make mathematical thinking into something that *all students* can expect to do in school.

Magdalene Lampert

Acknowledgments

The list of people who have inspired, shaped, and supported our work is long. There are many to thank. We start by acknowledging two math education giants upon whose shoulders we stand: Mark Driscoll and Magdalene Lampert. Mark Driscoll has taught us a great deal about thinking mathematically and ensuring that all students have a seat at the "math thinking" table. Not only has he shaped our ideas, he has shaped our professional lives. We are fortunate to call Mark our colleague, mentor, and friend. Magdalene Lampert understands, better than anyone, the complexities of ambitious teaching. From Magdalene, we have learned the power of routinizing instructional designs to support teacher practice and student learning. We have benefited from Magdalene's keen eye on the instructional routines we developed. Magdalene has become a champion of our work, and for that we are truly grateful.

We want to thank the many teachers who participated in various professional development sessions we led between 2010 and 2016. Your excitement, interest, questions, and pushback helped us to deconstruct the Standards for Mathematical Practice and construct a set of instructional routines that develop those practices in *all* students. We finally have the book! And we truly could not have written it without you.

We would like to acknowledge our colleagues, collaborating teachers, and math residents at BPE's Boston Teacher Residency (BTR) program. We are grateful to our residents who grabbed onto these routines with gusto and worked to make them their own. We would also like to thank the BTR collaborating teachers at the Orchard Gardens K–8 Pilot School, Maurice J. Tobin Elementary School, and Jeremiah E. Burke High School who supported the residents as they learned to lead routines in their classrooms.

We would like to acknowledge Danny Voloch and the math instructional specialists at New Visions for Public Schools in New York who embraced these routines, built them

into their Accessing Algebra through Inquiry Curriculum (a2i), and developed teacher facility with the routines. Their concrete vision for embedding routines in curriculum materials inspires us.

We would like to acknowledge Amy Brodesky and Harold Asturias whose work in math, targeting students with learning disabilities and English language learners, respectively, has significantly shaped our thinking and the design of the routines in this book.

We would like to thank Mary Eich for her long-standing and steadfast commitment to high-quality math instruction for all students. Her confidence in our work supported us as we embarked on this journey.

Our work with the math practices was jump-started when Life Legeros, then the Massachusetts state supervisor of mathematics, asked us to create the Developing Math Practices in Algebra (DMPA) course. We would like to thank Life for getting us started unpacking the math practices. In addition, we'd like to acknowledge our DMPA course facilitators, Cathy Anasauskas, Patti Aube, Robin Bergen, Matthew Costa, Kathy Foulser, Ellie Goldberg, YeukSze Leong, and Chris Ricard, who worked with us at the very beginning to make sense of the math practice standards.

Several people helped with the writing of this book. We extend a big thank-you to all the folks at Heinemann, who helped get this book out the door. In particular, we would like to thank Katherine Bryant, our editor, who worked hard to understand our ideas and even harder to help us communicate them clearly and concisely. She answered our many questions and provided guidance and reasoned feedback every step of the way. We would also like to thank Julie Biggane and Liz Ramirez, two extraordinary New York City public school math educators, for reviewing drafts and providing insightful feedback. Their input made the book that much better.

Finally, we would like to say a special thank-you to our families, Lorraine, McKenna, Dennis, Katie, Conor, Ryan, Doug, Evan, and Alix. This has been a long process and their support throughout has kept us persevering and writing. Thank you.

Preface

When the Common Core State Standards for Mathematics were released, we were knee-deep in supporting teachers as they embarked upon the challenge of making sense of students' mathematical thinking. We were fortunate to have the vision and work of Mark Driscoll and his colleagues at Education Development Center (EDC) as a basis for informing our work. Mark had articulated algebraic habits of mind and geometric habits of mind, and we had worked with him on those projects as well as others that came before them. That work included naming key ideas of both algebraic and geometric thinking and finding images of them in students' mathematical thinking. We were now working with middle school teachers to develop these habits of mind in students. It seemed like a natural transition to begin trying to apply a similar process to the Common Core standards for mathematical practice—naming key ideas and finding images of them in students' mathematical thinking. However, the task proved to be much less simple than that.

We spent considerable time unpacking the descriptions of the math practices, then worked to share them with teachers in ways that modeled ambitious teaching. It was our philosophy that the most effective way to unpack the math practices with teachers was to engage them in the practices as learners, so we felt that we needed to implement the same kind of instructional practices that we know to be effective with students. When teachers experienced the ways in which we were modeling teaching, many of them decided to engage their students in similar ways. They came back to us reporting that students who often struggle were surpassing all of their expectations. In particular, they noted that students who were typically not engaging in math class were increasingly participating in ways that they had not before. These results caused us to look more carefully at the pedagogies that were built into these learning experiences and to make those

pedagogies explicit to teachers. We began to realize that if these pedagogies were not in place, then students, particularly students with learning disabilities and English language learners, would not have access to developing the mathematical practices. And our biggest fear was that the achievement gap that exists would become deeper and wider.

As we were beginning to define activities that used these pedagogies that teachers could implement in their classrooms, Magdalene Lampert's work (Lampert and Graziani 2009; Lampert et al. 2010) with "instructional activity structures" was percolating. Magdalene arrived on the scene at the Boston Teacher Residency program in the Boston public schools, sharing her vision for these structured designs for learning. She had reason to believe that such structures would provide novice teachers with a specific framework that would help them learn to teach ambitiously, to engage students in high levels of thinking and reasoning, while supporting all learners. We saw a parallel between being a novice teacher learning new teaching practices—the focus of Magdalene's work— and being an experienced teacher learning to implement new teaching practices focused around the math practices—the focus of our work. So, we began to think about refining the activities we had developed into the instructional activity structures that Magdalene described. As such, we began to write "instructional routines" to foster the math practices in all students. (We refer to them as *routines*, and you'll read more about this in Chapter 2.) Although we understood from Magdalene's work that the instructional routines would support preservice and novice teachers, our work with experienced teachers indicated that *all* teachers appreciate and benefit from the supports the routines offered both teachers and students. We knew that the use of instructional routines was currently gaining some popularity in different subject areas. These routines were becoming a staple in small-group work in English language arts classrooms and more prevalent in elementary math lessons as more and more teachers used routines like Interactive Read-Aloud and Number Talks to support student learning. The routines in this book build on this emerging practice in English language arts and elementary math classrooms and use the predictability in instructional routines to develop students' habits of mathematical thinking. Each routine defines a framework or structure of "thinking steps" focused around specific sets of questions as a standard format that can be used with a range of mathematics content. Supports that are essential for students with learning disabilities and English language learners serve to engage all students in developing mathematical thinking. Of course, developing mathematical thinking and reasoning takes time and requires multiple opportunities; that's why it's important that these routines become routine for students. Teaching students to think and reason is perhaps the greatest challenge we face as math educators, and these routines provide clear pathways to do so.

In Chapters 1 and 2, respectively, we provide our framework for thinking about the Standards for Mathematical Practice as well as essential background information and framing of the instructional routines, so we strongly recommend that you read these first. However, you may choose to focus on Chapters 3, 4, 5, and 6 in any order. The final chapter (7), transitions from getting to know the routines to implementing the routines in your classroom. As you integrate the instructional routines into your students' learning experiences, we are certain you'll be pleased with the results!

Using the Math Practices as a Means to Provide Access to Rich Mathematical Reasoning

Ms. King sat in her mathematics department meeting and heaved a quiet, personal sigh. They were discussing their current curriculum map, recently completed to better align with the Common Core State Standards (CCSS), and how to best include the Standards for Mathematical Practice throughout the curriculum. Although Ms. King believed in the intent and purpose of the math practices and saw their importance in her students' mathematics learning, all she could think about was how potentially difficult it seemed for many of her students to realize these practices. A number of her students struggled with learning disabilities, not to mention those who did not have an identified disability but still just struggled with mathematics. And two of her groups had a number of students who were English language learners (ELLs) at various levels of fluency. *Maybe I can just focus first on the content standards that are new to my grade,* she thought to herself, *and maybe start with one of the easier math practices.*

Why Should I Pay Attention to the Math Practices?

It can be daunting to think about helping *all* students both meet the mathematics content standards for their grade level and also develop their mathematical reasoning ability as described in the eight standards for mathematical practice. There is a strong temptation to put the math practices on the back burner in service of meeting the content standards or to choose one or two of the math practices that seem easier in some way for students to achieve and teachers to infuse into their instruction.

We're here to argue that there are two very compelling reasons to pay attention to the math practices, whether or not your state has adopted the CCSS. The first is that the eight standards for mathematical practice articulated in the CCSS for Mathematics beautifully summarize the ways mathematicians work. They describe the ways effective math doers think and the kinds of actions they take when engaged in mathematical problem solving. Although these are not new and different ideas, they provide a more specific and complete description of what it means to "do mathematics" than our profession has had in the past. They represent our profession's most recent articulation of mathematical sense-making and problem solving. As such, they provide us with new descriptions of how our students should be interacting with mathematics in our classrooms.

The second reason is that we believe that the math practices provide untapped opportunities for students to engage in rich mathematical reasoning. Rather than being a barrier to those who "can't," in particular ELLs and students with learning disabilities (SWLDs), the practices actually provide access and opportunity for *all* students to engage successfully with mathematics. This belief is based on several years of work using the tools and resources that we will share with you in this book and that have proven successful in numerous classrooms filled with a wide range of learners.

So this book was written not only to share our passion for the vision of doing mathematics that is captured in the practice standards, but also to share some practical and tested ways to bring those kinds of practices to life in your mathematics classroom, with students who may not have had a lot of success with mathematics as well as with those students who have. We encourage you to take the time in Chapters 1 and 2 of this book to understand the different roles that the math practice standards can have in students' mathematical reasoning and how our instructional routines are designed to develop the math practices. The later chapters will then lay out a set of those instructional routines.

Not All Math Practices Are Created Equal

A quick scan of the CCSS will reveal that the eight standards for mathematical practice are numbered and appear in the same order whenever they are referenced throughout the CCSS:

CCSS Standards for Mathematical Practice (2010)

1. Make sense of problems and persevere in solving them.
2. Reason abstractly and quantitatively.
3. Construct viable arguments and critique the reasoning of others.
4. Model with mathematics.
5. Use appropriate tools strategically.
6. Attend to precision.
7. Look for and make use of structure.
8. Look for and express regularity in repeated reasoning.

Each of them is described in a paragraph, with no indication of relative importance or weight. It's probably a safe bet to say that if we asked which of the eight math practices is most important, the answer would be "They are *all* important," that the numbers exist simply to let us know there are eight math practices and are not meant to imply a certain hierarchy.

Yet that answer provides little or no guidance about how to begin to incorporate them into instruction or help students begin to learn to use them in their own mathematical reasoning. In our work with teachers over the past six years, some distinct differences between the practices have become increasingly clear. Some of the practices have captured important avenues of mathematical thinking in a problem, while other practices have articulated critical supports to those avenues of thinking. Figure 1.1 summarizes these roles for the practices that we'll propose in the next sections.

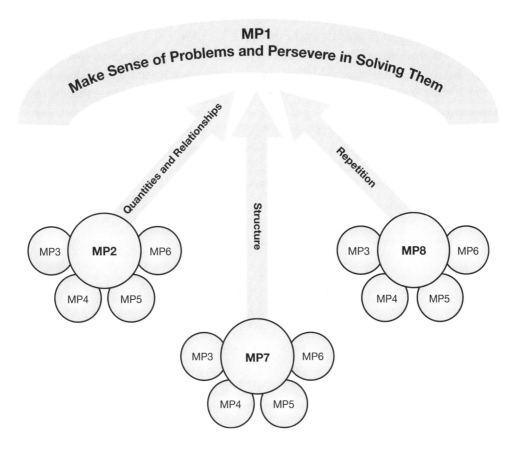

Figure 1.1 Diagram that shows the relationship of the practices to each other

The "Lead Actors" (Math Practices 1, 2, 7, and 8)

You'll notice in the figure that four of the practices sit either in the overarching banner across the top of all the other practices or in larger circles than the others. We like to think of the eight math practices in terms of "lead actors" and "supporting actors" in students' mathematical reasoning, and these four math practices are our lead actors (Figure 1.1):

- Math practice (MP) 1: Make sense of problems and persevere in solving them.
- MP2: Reason abstractly and quantitatively.
- MP7: Look for and make use of structure.
- MP8: Look for and express regularity in repeated reasoning.

Calling them *lead actors* does not mean these practices are more important than the others; rather, it describes their leading role in students' mathematical reasoning. These practices focus on ways for students to successfully enter and remain engaged in mathematical reasoning, and as such, they "lead" the way in students' reasoning.

MP1: *Make Sense of Problems and Persevere in Solving Them*

Make sense of problems and persevere in solving them (MP1) is an overarching goal, developing what the National Council of Teachers of Mathematics Teaching Practices call "productive struggle in mathematics." This math practice emphasizes sense making and perseverance and is one of our lead actors because of the necessity of this overarching goal to students' success in mathematics. All the other math practices sit in service of this goal, because if a student gives up, there is no opportunity for any other mathematical thinking to occur. Students engage in this practice as they make sense of a problem, comprehend the question, consider the context, identify important information, formulate and enact a plan, then refine and justify their work. Perseverance develops when students feel as though they have a way into the problem and other approaches to try when their initial solution strategy comes to a dead end.

MP2, MP7, and MP8: *Avenues of Thinking*

The additional lead actors—*reason abstractly and quantitatively* (MP2), *look for and make use of structure* (MP7), and *look for and express regularity in repeated reasoning* (MP8)— describe three different avenues of mathematical thinking that provide entry into and through all kinds of math problems. Each of these three lead practices calls for attention to a different mathematical aspect of the problem, is driven by different wonderings, and results in different problem-solving actions. One avenue of thinking may be better suited for a particular problem than another. One avenue might lead into or grow out of another. Taken together, they become a powerful problem-solving toolbox. We will delve deeper into MP2, MP7, MP8, and MP1 as they relate to specific instructional routines in Chapters 3, 4, 5, and 6, respectively. For now, let's look briefly at each of these three lead practices, their key ideas, and what they suggest for how someone using this line of reasoning might enter and work through a math problem.

Different Avenues of Mathematical Thinking

Imagine three students—Quinn, Stephanie, and Roberto—are given the following problem (Massachusetts Comprehensive Assessment System 2014):

> Jeanie has a goal to run a total of 800 laps around her school's track this year. Her plan is to run exactly 4 laps each day.
>
> Which of the following expressions represents the total number of laps Jeanie will have left to run after d days?
>
> A. $800 - 4d$
>
> B. $800d - 4$
>
> C. $4d - 800$
>
> D. $4 - 800d$

Quinn: *Reason abstractly and quantitatively (MP2)*

Quinn reads the problem once and starts wondering, "What are the important quantities in this situation?" He rereads the problem, this time paying attention to the information about quantities, things that can be counted or measured, thinking, *So this is about numbers of laps and numbers of days, number of laps total, number of laps run, and number of laps left to run.* Quinn then wonders, *How could I represent these so I can see how they're related?* Quinn makes a diagram (Figure 1.2), with the total 800 laps as a horizontal bar, and squares of 4 underneath for the number of laps run each day. Because he doesn't know how many days Jeanie has run, he just draws a few to get the gist of the problem. Creating the diagram helps him to see that the remaining laps can be represented by the shaded portion of the diagram.

The diagram helps him see that an expression for the shaded portion (the difference between the total number of

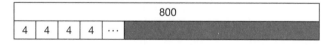

Figure 1.2

laps she wants to run and the 4 laps per day she has already run) is choice A: $800 - 4d$.

The process of diagramming helped Quinn see how the number of laps left to run is related to the total number of laps and the number of laps already run, which helped him select the correct algebraic representation. Quinn was reasoning abstractly and quantitatively.

Students entering a problem through this avenue of thinking will attend to the quantities and relationships in the problem situation. They ask themselves questions like:

- *What are the important quantities and relationships in this situation?*
- *How are the quantities related?*
- *How can I represent the situation so I see the relationships/quantities?*
- *Is there a quantity not stated but implied in the problem—a "hidden" quantity—that can help me solve this?*

They often take actions such as listing out quantities and relationships in a problem statement or making a table or diagram to see or bring to the surface any mathematical relationships.

Stephanie: *Look for and make use of structure (MP7)*

Stephanie approaches the problem differently than Quinn. Stephanie reads the problem, then reads it again and thinks, *What's going on in this situation? Is this behaving like another problem I've seen?* She recognizes this problem as a part/total problem in which she knows something about the "total"—she knows the total number of laps. She also knows something about the "parts"—4 laps per day—but realizes she's missing one piece of essential information that makes up the remaining "part." She reasons that if she's looking for what's left after something happens, then she's looking for a difference, and she could subtract from the total. Considering the "4 laps each day," Stephanie writes $4 + 4 + 4 + 4 +$ . . . and knows she can rewrite that as $4d$, where d is the number of days. She looks at the four choices for expressions and sees that all of them have two mathematical "chunks" separated by an operation sign and all involve subtraction. She remembers that you have to be careful when subtracting because order matters. She reasons that to find the remaining laps, she has to subtract the number of laps already run from the total number of laps, so she selects choice A: $800 - 4d$.

Stephanie could mentally "step back" from the problem to notice the mathematical chunks and the operations being used on them, as well as focusing on the details of the expressions. Throughout her problem solving, she was surfacing and leveraging the mathematical structure of the expressions to solve the problem.

When students approach problem solving through a structural avenue of thinking, they pay attention to how mathematical situations behave: the types of numbers or kinds of objects involved and the rules and properties that govern those numbers and objects. When they are thinking structurally, they ask themselves questions like:

- *What type of problem is this?*
- *How is this situation behaving? Can I connect it to something else I know?*

- *How can I use properties to uncover hidden structure?*
- *What's another way to write this (number, expression, and so on) that might be more helpful?*
- *How can I get the answer without doing all those calculations?*

Paying attention to structure means you take problem-solving actions like breaking complicated objects (e.g., expressions, visuals, and so on) into chunks. You look for and make connections between disparate objects. You change the form of numbers and expressions and transform space to help you make sense.

Roberto: Look for and express regularity in repeated reasoning (MP8)

Roberto thinks about the problem differently than both Quinn and Stephanie. Roberto starts by trying some numbers to see how the situation is working. Because he's still exploring and not trying to find the answer just yet, he substitutes numbers that are easy to calculate with, even though they may be unlikely candidates for the final answer. He records the following on his paper.

What if J runs 10 days?	What if J runs 100 days?	What if J runs 50 days?
$4 \times 10 = 40$	$4 \times 100 = 400$	$4 \times 50 = 200$
$800 - 40 = 760$	$800 - 400 = 400$	$800 - 200 = 600$

Figure 1.3

Roberto notices that every time he tries a number, he ends up doing the same steps: multiplying the number of days by 4, then subtracting that product from 800. Noticing this repetition leads him to choose answer A: $800 - 4d$.

Note that Roberto's attention is not on refining the number he is testing—10 or 100 or 50—to narrow in on the right answer, but instead is on the operations and what he is doing *to* the numbers. He is sensing the "mathematical rhythm" that repeats in each of his attempts: "multiply by 4, subtract from 800; multiply by 4, subtract from 800; multiply by 4, subtract from 800. . . ." Roberto is reasoning through repetition.

Students who take the repeated reasoning avenue of thinking attend to repetition in calculations or processes. They ask themselves questions like:

- *Do I keep doing the same thing over and over again?*
- *Am I drawing or building or counting or calculating in the same way each time?*
- *What about this process is repeating?*
- *How can I use the repetition to make my rule?*

Paying attention to repetition requires students to keep a record of their process. In Roberto's case, he recorded his calculations, not just the final "answer" (e.g., 760 laps are left after 10 days of running) because repetition in "repeated reasoning" is found in the process, not the result. Students who reason this way may try several numbers and track their calculations. Other problems might call for building or drawing or constructing several figures and attending to *that* process. This approach requires that students simultaneously maintain oversight of their process while attending to the details of the repeated steps. The final action is often to generalize the steps of the repetition, as Roberto did.

Each student arrived at the same correct answer, but each approached the problem a different way. They each paid attention to different aspects of the problem, and different internal questions drove their problem solving. This difference in attention and driving questions led to different problem-solving actions. In essence, they were each traveling down a different mathematical avenue of thinking. This information is summarized in a table in Appendix A.

Do you find yourself gravitating more toward one of these avenues than another? Most do. And your students will too. However, even though one avenue may feel more comfortable than another, it is crucial that students develop facility with all three of these types of thinking if they are to develop the tenacity it takes to persevere through complex math problems where problem-solving dead ends or computational road blocks require problem solvers to try another avenue. And in reality, anyone doing mathematics does not use these avenues of thinking so separately from each other. Using one line of thinking can point to another, providing a new insight better explored through a different line of reasoning, or supported by a second line of reasoning. For example, Roberto's initial questions of *What about this process is repeating?* and *How can I use the repetition to make my rule?* could easily lead to his wondering *How do the quantities relate to each other?* (MP2) or *How is this (situation, object, process, etc.) behaving? Can I connect it to something else I know?* (MP7).

The Supporting Actors (MP3, MP4, MP5, MP6)

Although the leading practices define ways of thinking mathematically in a problem, the remaining practices describe important ways to navigate down each avenue: paying attention to the validity of your or another's reasoning, selectively choosing and implementing useful tools, modeling, and gauging your need for precision. These supporting actors (MP3, MP4, MP5, and MP6) play important roles in the problem-solving process no matter which avenue of thinking you take (Figure 1.1), so they appear under all three.

The supporting actors in the math practices are:

- MP3: Construct viable arguments and critique the reasoning of others.
- MP4: Model with mathematics.
- MP5: Use appropriate tools strategically.
- MP6: Attend to precision.

MP3: *Construct viable arguments and critique the reasoning of others*

Regardless of the avenue of thinking you take into a problem, you must stop along the way to convince yourself and be prepared to convince others that your approach is reasonable and your solution makes sense. For Quinn, that might mean making the case for which quantities are important to pay attention to and being able to show that he has accurately included all the important problem information in his diagram. For Stephanie, it means connecting the two parts she saw in the problem statement (the 800 total laps and the 4 laps each day) to the two chunks in the algebraic expression and communicating what she knows about how multiplication and subtraction work. Finally, for Roberto, it means convincing himself that no matter what number of days he tries, he is always going to be quadrupling that number and subtracting it from 800. All three would need to craft and communicate convincing claims and consider each other's work. Their communication would involve not just listing the steps they followed, but sharing the reasoning behind their approach, including what they thought was important to pay attention to, and why, as well as the questions they asked themselves that drove their investigations. This is at the heart of constructing arguments and critiquing reasoning.

MP4: *Model with mathematics*

Model with mathematics (MP4) means actively thinking about what mathematics can be used to make sense of and solve a real-world problem. If you are thinking structurally, you are often trying to make sense of how a problem situation is behaving and to think about a mathematical concept that behaves in the same way and thus can be used to model the situation. Stephanie does this when she recognizes that subtraction is relevant. For Quinn, modeling with mathematics may have come into play after he made sense of the problem by considering the important quantities and relationships and chose to model them with a diagram. Whether you are reasoning about quantities, thinking structurally, or even reasoning with repetition, you will often find yourself connecting the problem at hand to mathematics you know and then using that math to find a solution. And when you shift to using that math to find a solution, you are modeling with mathematics.

MP5: *Use appropriate tools strategically*

Often when we think of tools in the math classroom, we think of manipulatives and technology. The CCSS for Mathematics asks us to expand our view of tools beyond calculators and compasses to consider such mathematical tools as number lines, diagrams, graphs, and tables. We are asked to think about, for example, the strategic ways we can use color or shading in our math work. Quinn's approach provides an example of both these ideas, as Quinn chose to use a diagram as a tool to see the important quantities and color to help highlight relationships in the problem.

You might have just read that sentence and thought, "Wait a minute, you just said that Quinn was modeling with mathematics when he made the diagram! Now you're saying the diagram was a tool!" Yes we did. The diagram in Figure 1.2 could be a manifestation of MP4 or MP5; it all depends on the intention of the math doer. Was Quinn thinking, *This is one of those diagramming problems*, or was he thinking, *What tool could I use to help me see the relationships between the quantities?* It's not important whether we label Quinn's use of a diagram with the right math practice. What is important is that we develop students' capacity to think about the math and the tools they can bring to bear on their problem solving.

MP6: *Attend to precision*

MP6 refers to precision in both your math-doing and your communication of ideas. It's important to think beyond correct calculations and math vocabulary use. *Attend to precision* means developing a sense of how precise you need to be in your work. Can you make a quick sketch of the graph to see the behavior of the function, or do you need to plot points more precisely to see, for example, the point of intersection between two functions? Do you need to calculate the exact value of an expression or just enough to know that the value is greater than 50? When looking for repetition in calculations, like Roberto was doing, you often need a lower degree of precision, because you are focusing on the repetition in the operations, not the resultant numeric values. When reasoning quantitatively and constructing a diagram as Quinn did, you need to be precise enough so that you can see relationships between quantities, but your diagram does not need to be exact and perfectly labeled. A greater degree of precision and complete labels would be important if you were using the diagram to communicate your solution to someone else. Just as students need to think strategically about the tools they use when problem solving, students must build the habit of considering the appropriate level of precision for their math-doing.

Now that we've summarized the relationships among the practices, let's look at how the actions that accompany the math practices actually provide access to a wide range of learners and learning styles.

Using the Math Practices as Opportunities, Not Hurdles

We are convinced that the ways in which the math practices ask students to engage in the math doing actually create opportunities for *all* math learners, in particular SWLDs and ELLs, our "special populations" for the purpose of this book—even though this may seem counterintuitive because the math practices challenge students to think and reason in sophisticated and mathematically demanding ways in the context of complex mathematical tasks. Let's examine why.

The Overlapping Needs of Special Populations

SWLDs and ELLs have a particular set of learning needs in mathematics. The literature suggests that SWLDs need mathematics learning experiences that:

- provide authentic, meaningful contexts
- model learning strategies using multisensory techniques
- provide students with opportunities to use language to describe their understanding
- provide multiple practice opportunities. (Van Garderen 2007; Allsopp et al. 2003; Baxter et al. 2002; Gersten et al. 2009)

SWLDs benefit most from explicit instruction, opportunities to verbalize their mathematical reasoning, visual representations, and a range and sequence of mathematics examples (Gersten et al. 2009). Gersten et al. (2008) cite strong evidence for the effectiveness of SWLDs' use of a "generic problem-solving guide in which the strategy (list of steps) is not problem-specific." Similarly, ELLs need mathematics experiences that:

- connect mathematics with their own life experiences and existing knowledge
- use visual supports such as concrete objects, videos, illustrations, and gestures
- provide ample opportunity to connect language to mathematical representations such as tables, graphs, equations, or diagrams
- include discussion of students' mathematical reasoning through their writing and problem solving. (Chval and Chavez 2011; Furner, Noorchaya, and Duffy 2005; Zahner 2012; Ng and Lee 2009; Chval and Khisty 2009)

There is clear overlap between the instructional recommendations for these two populations. Both sets of recommendations point toward:

- use of authentic contexts
- use of multimodal techniques
- rich opportunities for language use embedded in mathematical learning experiences
- instruction that scaffolds students' development of increasingly abstract thinking.

And it gets even better. These four areas of common need reveal a great deal of overlap with the approaches to doing mathematics that are championed in the standards for mathematical practice!

- **Use of authentic contexts:** Making sense of problems and persevering in solving them (MP1) is all about students making sense of problem situations, many of which are set in authentic contexts. When students reason abstractly and quantitatively (MP2), authentic contexts are implied as they "decontextualize" and "contextualize"—moving fluidly back and forth between disconnecting the numbers from the problem context to explore some part of the mathematics, then returning to the context as they figure out what their results mean in terms of that context. Finally, modeling with mathematics (MP4) is based on the need for all students to be able to "apply the mathematics they know to solve problems arising in everyday life, society, and the work place."

- **Use of multimodal techniques:** If you look across all the math practices as a collection, you see a host of multisensory approaches suggested. The descriptions of MP1 and MP3 in the CCSS document make reference to use of concrete objects, pictures, drawings, diagrams, or actions. MP2 and MP7 support the creation of visuals and connecting representations. MP3 and MP6 place a premium on students communicating their thinking orally and in writing. Students who look for and express regularity in repeated reasoning (MP8) recognize that repetition by physically acting out a situation or by moving manipulatives or by drawing subsequent figures: they can hear the repetition when working with a partner or in a small group, and they can see the repetition in repeated calculations they record.

- **Opportunities for language use:** The clearest place where this emerges is in MP3, construct viable arguments and critique the reasoning of others. However, MP1 calls on students to explain correspondences between different representations, and MP6 focuses on developing precision in students' communication. Taken together, these practices paint a picture of a discourse-rich classroom where students co-construct ideas, craft convincing arguments, and critique the reasoning of others. This dovetails with the National Council of Teachers of Mathematics Teaching Practice that calls on teachers to *facilitate meaningful mathematical discourse*.

- **Scaffolds for increasingly abstract thinking:** The mathematical practices are not found in the answers to math problems; they come to life in students' thinking and reasoning as they try to make sense of a problem and in the various tools and resources they draw on. A natural first step in this sense making is to work with the specific context at hand. This may mean using manipulatives or other realia (real-life objects and materials) to model the situation, so that a generalizable repetition or underlying structure can emerge. It may mean representing the important problem quantities visually with a diagram, graph, or table to surface relationships between those quantities that can be leveraged to form a rule. It may mean running a bunch of numbers through the problem situation to capture repetition in a calculation that can then be generalized with variables. In all of these approaches, students have stepping stones as they move toward the abstract generalization. Research suggests that a trajectory from concrete to representational to abstract is critical in particular for struggling learners.

Five Guiding Principles of Instruction That Promote the Math Practices

Given this commonality in the needs of both ELLs and SWLDs, we believe it's possible to have an approach to instruction that supports both populations simultaneously (and other students as well) in learning to make use of the math practices. The key lies in:

- taking an approach to instruction that capitalizes on the many characteristics of the math practices that align with these best instructional practices for supporting ELLs and SWLDs

- intentionally cultivating students' perseverance in problem solving by developing their facility with the three avenues of mathematical thinking described in the lead practices

- developing students' facility with the supporting practices as part of their mathematics toolkit to draw on when using one or more of the three avenues of mathematical thinking.

To understand what this approach looks like, let's start by looking at five underlying principles.

1. High cognitive demand
2. Multimodal learning
3. A language-rich environment
4. Building on students' learning strengths
5. Growth mind-set

High Cognitive Demand

The math practices live not in the final answer a student gets for a math problem, but in the thinking and reasoning a student uses to arrive at a solution, so students need mathematics tasks that encourage them to think and reason. For example, consider the difference in asking students to find the mean of the data set {9, 10, 8, 4, 6, 2} (low cognitive demand) or instead to find two different sets of six data points that both have a mean of 6.5 (moderate cognitive demand). The cognitive demand of this task can be raised further by asking students to determine the validity of the following line of reasoning: McKenna knows that the average age of all the large dogs at the Doggie Daycare center is 6.2 years and the average age of all the small dogs at the center is 8.8 years. She says that she can quickly determine the average age of all the dogs by finding the mean of 6.2 and 8.8 (i.e., 7.5) (high cognitive demand). These kinds of tasks provide students with an opportunity to think and reason mathematically. If students are not given high-demand problem situations with which to grapple, they will not need to think and reason mathematically.

Simply put, they will have no need—and no opportunity—to use the math practices.

In service of making mathematics accessible to students who struggle, it is sometimes common for teachers to focus almost exclusively on skills development and break instruction down into small discrete steps to be memorized and repeated (i.e., low demand tasks). Although these supports have an important place in students' learning, it is a disservice to these students to not also provide them with opportunities to engage in higher-demand thinking; special populations of students need this opportunity to build conceptual understanding and to engage in mathematical sense making and discourse. Teachers can instead provide a broader range of opportunities for struggling students, using instructional routines and the practices as "inroads" for students to have access to higher-demand work. The instructional routines in this book are designed to engage students in cognitively demanding work and support *all* students' entry into and ongoing engagement with the use and development of the math practices.

Multimodal Learning Experiences

All students can benefit from building the capacity to explore and communicate mathematics using a range of modalities—visual, auditory, kinesthetic, and tactile. For example, to look for and express regularity in repeated reasoning, students must learn to identify the repetition in a problem situation. This mathematical repetition can be felt tangibly or seen concretely as students move manipulatives or build with chips. It can be heard when students listen to each other describe their calculations or the process of a problem situation. Students can also draw on multiple modalities when they reason abstractly and quantitatively. As students learn to tease out relationships between important quantities in problem situations, they can act out the problem context (concrete), represent important quantities and relationships in the context in a diagram (representational), and connect the numbers, words, and visual to an algebraic expression or equation (abstract), providing entry points to a range of math learners.

Although a multimodal learning environment is important for all students, we believe it is perhaps the greatest lever for fostering the math practices especially in SWLDs and ELLs, serving as a critical component to circumventing learning and language barriers. Multimodal instruction allows students both to have a range of ways to process the information and to experience a concrete-representational-abstract approach to learning, both of which are high-leverage support strategies for SWLDs. Both strategies allow SWLDs to rely on a learning strength, such as strength in visual-spatial processing, or in kinesthetic learning. Multimodal instruction for ELLs, such as providing and discussing multiple representations, provide them access to and support for the production of language in the math classroom. Pointing to a diagram or showing a three-dimensional model or moving manipulatives not only makes student thinking visible, but also provides scaffolding for academic language use as a student can point to features of a visual for which she doesn't yet know the word or can move an object in a way she might not yet be able to describe verbally.

However, the standards for mathematical practice require *all* students to build the capacity to explore and communicate mathematics using a range of modalities if they are to be mathematically proficient. Therefore, the use of multiple modalities in instruction is not just to provide access to struggling students; a range of modalities provides all students the opportunity to work and think mathematically.

Language-Rich Environment

Language-rich mathematics classrooms are essential environments in which to develop mathematical understanding and practices. Phil Daro (2012) talks about how knowledge, cognition, and language are all threads of a single fabric of learning that develop together and progressively, and as ideas and relationships become more complex, so does language. Students begin sense making by verbalizing their thoughts in their own language, however incomplete or imprecise, and then moving toward more mathematical ways of communicating their ideas. In the process, not only does the language get more precise, but the mathematical ideas do as well. Providing opportunities through instructional techniques such as think-pair-share and turn-and-talks is not only critical to student sense making, it is essential to developing two of the math practices—*construct viable arguments and critique the reasoning of others* and *attend to precision*. Therefore students need multiple and varied experiences communicating mathematical thinking to themselves, each other, and an external audience.

As we noted earlier, research suggests that language-rich learning environments support the math learning of both SWLDs and ELLs. Research shows that students with learning difficulties who regularly express their math reasoning verbally show increased math performance (Gersten et al. 2008, 11). This self-talk—including asking oneself guiding questions while problem solving—appears to focus student attention on the task at hand, something especially helpful to many SWLDs. It also makes a student's thinking public, a byproduct that teachers can capitalize on during instruction.

It goes without saying that if English learners are to increase their language production, they need continuous opportunities to hear and produce academic language. However, pushing for precision in language when an English learner is just beginning to formulate a math idea can shut down the thinking process. Yet, not requiring students to, at some point, communicate their mathematical ideas in clear, complete, and convincing language limits their mathematical proficiency. So the use of academic language is not a question of *if*, but *when*. The challenge is to balance for students the mathematical cognitive demand with the linguistic cognitive load; in other words, be particularly aware of the balance between the demands of mathematical thinking and reasoning, and the stresses of processing and producing the language.

Building on Learning Strengths

Particularly in mathematics, where the emphasis can so often be on correct answers, it is easy to focus almost exclusively on students' learning weaknesses, on correcting their deficits. However, effective instruction that promotes the math practices includes mathematical experiences that build on a student's learning strengths and uses those strengths to address common student learning weaknesses. For example, when a teacher works with a student who has a verbal processing strength, she may choose to project expressions or equations alongside verbal descriptions. The teacher does not abandon the expressions or equations, but rather builds the student's capacity to interpret the expressions or equations by drawing on the student's verbal learning strength. Therefore, it is at least as important to pay attention to what a student *can* do as to what a student *cannot* do.

To build on students' learning strengths to help them develop the math practices, it is essential to get to know students as learners—not only the *content* they already know, but also *how* they learn and think best. Teachers can then plan support strategies that play to those strengths so that students can develop mathematical practices. The eight math practice standards illustrate habits of mathematical thinking that are broad and varied and that collectively describe a powerful suite of interrelated problem-solving capacities. This range of capacities invites multiple entry points into problem solving and therefore provides many opportunities to find a point of strength for a student and build from there.

Growth Mind-Set

Effective instruction that promotes the math practices fosters in students the ability to see mathematics as interconnected and sensible, and therefore doable with effort. When our focus shifts from a problem's answer to the various solution strategies and the thinking that leads to those strategies, students begin to see that mathematics not only makes sense but is learnable. Understanding what is happening "behind the curtain" takes the mystery out of the mathematics and allows for a growth mind-set.

SWLDs and ELLs all too often lack opportunities to see the interconnectedness, power, and beauty of mathematics, as their math learning experiences can tend to emphasize memorizing and practicing bite-size skills. For example, when language is a challenge, a default instructional approach is to show and have the student replicate. Although this approach may be effective for building skills, it falls short when the goal is to build conceptual understanding and language production. It also does not allow for math practice development. Teachers of SWLDs often support their students by providing them with explicit step-by-step problem-specific instruction. Research shows that this type of intervention leads to increased mastery of particular skills and procedures (Gersten et al. 2008). However, if this approach makes up the bulk of student learning experiences, students risk viewing mathematics as a series of unrelated topics, rules, and procedures with each new lesson bringing a new silo of information. Instruction in which the teacher does the thinking by creating and choosing the problem-solving tools and in which the student does the calculating can result in students becoming dependent on the teacher to suggest the right tool for the job, putting the teacher in the role of the GPS, telling the student what to do at every turn. Instead, teachers who are in the role of the compass, pointing the student in a fruitful problem-solving direction and reorienting as necessary, can begin to foster the math practices in their students.

Addressing the Challenge Through the Use of Instructional Routines

There is good news here for both teacher and students. These math practices that may have seemed daunting, or appeared as a barrier for those students who struggle in different ways with mathematics learning, actually provide a much-needed opportunity for all students to excel. To turn that opportunity into a practical reality, we have designed instructional routines based on the five guiding principles to develop and support students' use of these practices. Each routine is designed to emphasize the interconnectedness of mathematics and to provide a structure that helps students learn how to intentionally reason along a different avenue of mathematical thinking. As such, these routines are not problem-specific, they are "thinking-specific"; directions to students within the routines help keep the focus on different avenues of thinking. These instructional routines and strategies have been successfully implemented repeatedly in our work in a range of mathematics classrooms over the past six years. The next chapter presents an introduction to instructional routines and how they are universally designed to provide access to a wide range of math learners. In subsequent chapters, we'll introduce and discuss specific routines designed to foster individual math practices.

Instructional Routines

*A Vehicle for Developing Mathematical Practices
in All Students*

> "It is significant to realize that the most creative environments in
> our society are not the ever-changing ones. The artist's studio,
> the researcher's laboratory, the scholar's library are each kept
> deliberately simple so as to support the complexities of the work in
> progress. They are deliberately kept predictable so the unpredictable
> can happen."
>
> —**Lucy Calkins,** *Lessons from a Child*

The phrase *classroom routine* often conjures up images of time-saving procedures for classroom transitions. Teachers establish routines for entering the classroom ("Come in, sit down, take out your notebook, copy the date and the goal, and begin work"), passing in papers ("Place your homework in the left-hand side of your table folder and take today's class work out of the right hand side"), and ending class ("Take out your assignment books, copy tonight's homework, and place your class work in the finished work tray on your way out the door"). As students become practiced in these routines, time on task increases and opportunities for student learning grow. These classroom routines share some common characteristics: they have a predictable set of steps; students practice them repeatedly until they are second nature to the running of the classroom; and once students are familiar with them, these routines make certain habitual tasks smoother and simpler to execute, because both the teacher and students can devote much less attention to executing them.

Now, imagine a routine focused not on classroom management procedures but on ways of thinking mathematically when faced with an unfamiliar problem. Like the management routines, these "mathematical thinking routines" also have a predictable set of actions that students learn and then practice repeatedly until they are second nature.

They may involve getting started with an unfamiliar mathematics problem, or looking for relationships between two seemingly unrelated mathematical representations, or seeking regularity in a collection of computations to create a generalized equation.

The primary difference between these instructional routines and classroom management routines is that while general classroom management routines are often designed to efficiently transition from one learning opportunity to the next, instructional routines are situated in the learning opportunity itself, providing students with a predictable frame for engaging with the content. As the organization of a particular part of a lesson becomes increasingly familiar over time, both the teacher and the students know what to expect and can move fluidly in and through that part of the lesson.

In this chapter, we'll describe in general how these instructional routines work, then the subsequent chapters will introduce you to a series of different instructional routines you can use to develop your students' use of some of the mathematical practices.

Why Use Instructional Routines to Develop the Math Practices?

Our instructional routines provide access to the mathematical practices in three key ways:

- They allow for a greater focus on learning.
- They help students and teachers build crucial mathematical thinking habits.
- They provide a wider range of learners with access to the development and use of the math practices.

A Greater Focus on Learning

When people are first learning to drive, they are faced with a million small details to attend to: when and how to adjust mirrors, how to operate headlights, how to operate wipers, how to operate the radio or music, finding money for tolls at an upcoming toll booth—and all this on top of the crucial skills of steering, accelerating, braking, and paying attention to the movements of other drivers around them. As drivers become more familiar with their vehicle and the act of driving, many of these small, repeated actions become automatic and require little attention or thought, allowing drivers to focus most of their attention (we hope!) on their own movement and the movement of other drivers around them. Instructional routines serve the same function: they make more predictable the design and flow of the learning experience: "What is it that I'm supposed to be doing?," "What question will I be asked next?," or "How will things work today in the lesson?" The predictable structure lets students pay less attention to those questions and more attention to the way in which they and their classmates are thinking about a particular math task.

For you as the teacher, the routines keep the flow of the mathematics instruction deliberately predictable so that, as you gain familiarity with them, you can better attend to the most unpredictable elements of your mathematics instruction: how your students are making sense of the mathematics.

Building Crucial Mathematical Thinking Habits

Developing a mathematical "practice" means making habitual a particular way of mathematical thinking, whether it is about attending to quantities and relationships, attending to the mathematical structure of a problem situation, or attending to repetition in the processes or calculations. Building these habits requires repeated practice. And that practice needs to follow a predictable framework. When an athlete works on improving skills, he or she practices the same movements again and again, until the movements become second nature, allowing the athlete to focus on different elements of the game, such as game strategy. Instructional routines focused on the math practices provide a structure that you and your students can practice again and again until the steps you follow, the thinking skills you use, and the questions you ask yourself become automatic, and all of you develop a disposition to think in ways that reflect the practices when faced with a new problem. We'll say more about this throughout this chapter as we explore examples.

Access for a Wide Range of Learners

In Chapter 1, we already talked a bit about what research tells us about best practices for struggling learners and about the centrality of our five guiding principles: having cognitively demanding tasks; the use of multimodal learning experiences; working in a language-rich environment; building on students' learning strengths; and structuring learning to develop growth mindsets. So how does doing all these things to develop and use the math practices in the context of a routine provide access for a wide range of learners?

- The instructional routines in this book are intended to be used, well, routinely! The growing predictability and familiarity of each routine help students build a growing repertoire of tools for tackling unfamiliar problems and build their confidence in being able to do the mathematics. This is especially valuable for those students who lack confidence that they can be successful at all in math class.

- The routines are structured to keep the instructional focus on developing the thinking—which is where the math practices emerge—rather than on focusing predominantly on getting an answer. When the focus remains on the thinking, there is more room for different students' ways of thinking to become part of the discussion. The routines help students work through their thinking, while still leaving room for students' individual thought processes to emerge.

- The routines provide a structure for both teacher and students that creates a language-rich environment, involves use of multiple modalities and representations, and structures ways for students to successfully participate in discussions around those representations and the thinking that underlies them.

And finally, the built-in, ample processing time makes room for learners who need different amounts of time to make sense of the mathematics, whether because of a language issue or a disability or just because they do, while still engaging those who have already "arrived" at a productive way to solve the problem.

We'll say much more about each of these points throughout this chapter, and in each of the specific routines in subsequent chapters.

Core Elements of the Instructional Routines

All the routines in this book are constructed out of seven core elements that embody the guiding principles introduced at the end of Chapter 1. These elements keep the target math practice front and center in the instructional routine and provide access for special populations. These elements are:

1. articulation of a math practice goal

2. individual think time

3. partner work

4. full-group discussion of ideas

5. final math practice reflection

6. access through multiple modalities and multiple representations

7. liberal use of math practice–focused prompts.

The first five core elements speak to the flow of the routine. Each routine begins with a clear statement of a math practice goal. Throughout the middle steps of each routine, students are given individual think time, they are asked to work with a partner, and their thinking is shared in the full group. The routine ends with students reflecting on what they have learned about the featured mathematical practice. The last two core elements (6, 7) can best be thought of as threads woven throughout the routine to keep the focus on the math practice and ensure access to the thinking for all students. You could do any of the initial five elements in a math class without ever touching on the math practices or in a way that would leave some students behind. The final two elements bind the structure together to give the routines their impact.

Let's look at each core element and how it supports student development of and provides access to the math practices.

Articulation of a Math Practice Goal

What do we mean by a "math practice" goal? Typically, lessons have some combination of a skills goal (e.g., students will be able to find the factors of a number, students will solve two-step equations in one variable, and so on) and/or a concept goal (e.g., students will understand slope as a constant rate of change, students will understand why we need common denominators when we add or subtract fractions, and so on). A math practice goal, on the other hand, is a *thinking* goal and describes how students will learn to reason mathematically about a problem. In Chapter 1, we talked about how math practice (MP) 2, MP7, and MP8 represent three distinct avenues of thinking into and through a math problem. The math practice goal clearly communicates a specific aspect of one of these avenues of thinking, such as:

- *I can generate a diagram that captures the important quantities and relationships in a problem in order to develop a solution strategy* (sample math practice goal with a focus on MP2).

- Learn to surface the underlying mathematical structure of a problem by asking yourself, *How can I use properties to uncover structure?* (sample math practice goal with a focus on MP7).

- Effective math doers look for repetition in their calculations to generalize a process (sample math practice goal with a focus on MP8).

Each of these goals is written in a slightly different way. Whichever way you choose, the key is that each goal is explicit about some aspect of the math practice and helps students understand what it is about mathematical reasoning that they are supposed to learn. Articulating a math practice goal provides the opportunity to explicitly name and create a common language around the productive mathematical thinking that all too often remains unidentified in the mathematics classroom. This focus on mathematical reasoning brings to life two of our guiding principles for math practice development: the regular use of cognitively demanding work, and fostering a view of mathematics as interconnected, making sense, and doable with effort.

As you read about particular routines in the following chapters, pay attention to the way in which math practice goals are framed and used to focus student engagement with the mathematics. You will see that a math practice goal is explicitly stated at the start of each instructional routine, referred to throughout, and revisited at the end during the final reflection. Having this type of goal may be unfamiliar for students, so using it as a touchstone throughout the routine will help keep the focus on developing the avenue of thinking. A frequently stated math practice goal will also help build a common language students can use to communicate the way in which they are making sense of a problem.

> As you read the instructional routines in the next several chapters, pay attention to when, and in what ways, you are prompted to revisit the math practice goal.

Individual Think Time

Whether presented with a word problem to interpret, a visual representation to decipher, or a calculation to consider, all students need time to think before responding to a teacher's question, talking with a partner, or following a classmate's strategy presented to the whole group. Without this individual think time, many students who might need time to think and formulate a response will defer to those classmates who they know will call out an answer or raise their hand quickly and be quickly called on to provide a response. This extra processing time is also crucial for special populations. Some students with learning difficulties need extra time to retrieve stored information. English learners need extra time to find the English words to explain their ideas. Thus, think time can give students the opportunity to circumvent potential learning weaknesses and build on their strengths, one of our guiding principles.

Students are first given private think time when the math task used with the routine is introduced. Whenever a teacher or classmate introduces a new representation, whether a visual or a calculation strategy, students are given a few moments to quietly and individually make sense of the problem. In addition, students are always provided with individual think time before working with a partner. Then, at the end of each math practice routine, students are provided with quiet writing time to reflect before sharing their learning with a classmate. In the routines, it is never a question of whether to provide individual think time, but rather how much individual think time to provide students at different points in different routines. You'll see this addressed in each of the routines in subsequent chapters.

> As you read the instructional routines in the next several chapters, pay attention to how much individual think time students are given, and when during the routine they have those opportunities.

Partner Work

Partner work regularly follows individual think time in these math practice routines. It provides students with regular practice in explaining their thinking and an opportunity to discuss each other's ideas to make sense of them. These two math communication skills are the bedrock of MP3: *Construct viable arguments and critique the reasoning of others*, and integral to the way students will build knowledge through their classroom discourse. In all the routines, partner work provides students with the opportunity to reflect on how both they and someone else started to make sense of a problem situation, which keeps the focus on the math practice avenue of thinking.

Providing time for students to work together with a partner is central to a language-rich environment, another of our guiding principles. Social learners, as well as students for whom auditory learning is a strength, benefit from time to talk through their math ideas with a partner. Partner work provides English language learners an opportunity to hear academic language modeled and a less stressful environment in which to practice their academic language production before being asked to share in the full group.

> As you read the instructional routines in the next several chapters, pay attention to when students are prompted to work with a partner and the focus of that partner work.

Whole-Class Discussion

In all these math practice routines, whole-class discussion follows individual think time and partner work. Students are better prepared to participate in a whole-class discussion after having an opportunity to process and develop their own thinking.

Students presenting in the full group are prompted to first share how they initially made sense of the task at hand, such as by identifying and representing important quantities in a problem situation, or connecting two disparate representations, or identifying regularity in a repeated process. Note that this is not the same as asking students to "explain what you did to solve the problem." Rather than focusing on the steps they followed, they are asked to share what they noticed mathematically about the problem and how that helped them decide on an approach to take. Each routine is structured to help students learn how to "notice mathematically" in different ways. The "ask-yourself" questions can be a useful tool for helping students understand how to talk about what they noticed mathematically.

Students are often asked to restate or paraphrase what another student said. There are often multiple passes at having students explain an idea, and these multiple passes are intentional. Those students who need additional processing time get to hear ideas explained more than once. Students for whom English is not their first language benefit from the repetition, giving them more time to sort out what is being said. The multiple passes also provide English language learners multiple opportunities for academic language production. And all students benefit from the exercise of having to restate or paraphrase the thinking of another student, because it causes students to make sense of it for themselves.

Multiple representations and multiple learning modalities play a central role in the whole-class discussions; we'll say more about this in the chapters that follow.

As you read through the routines in this book, consider the ways in which the whole-class discussions are structured to provide all students multiple examples of a particular math practice avenue of thinking and multiple passes to communicate clearly their mathematical thinking.

These three core elements make up the effective and broadly usable think-pair-share instructional strategy. All of the instructional routines follow an overarching think-pair-share flow as students move from individual think time into partner work and finally share out in the full group. But look closely and you will see this familiar flow repeated in smaller cycles throughout the routines. For example, the math practice reflection at the end of each routine is structured as a think (write)-pair-share. As you read through the routines in subsequent chapters, you will see that often when a new approach or representation is shared in the whole-class discussion, the teacher pauses the class for some individual processing time, then prompts students to turn to a partner and quickly discuss how they are making sense of the shared idea before discussing the approach in the full group.

So why so much thinking, pairing, and sharing? Because purposefully combining individual, partner, and whole-group interaction supports a range of learners by creating opportunities and varied structures for them to process their mathematical ideas and their learning as well as the mathematical ideas of others.

Math Practice Reflection

Rather than asking students for general reflections at the end of the routine (e.g., "What did you learn today?" or "What's one question you have?"), math practice–focused reflections include sentence starters and frames to focus students' reflection on the featured math practice, such as:

- "When thinking structurally, I have learned to ask myself _____ because _____."
- "One way to see the relationship between two quantities is to _____."
- "One way to recognize repetition is to _____."
- "When reading a word problem, it is important to pay attention to _____."

The math practice reflection is structured the same way in each routine:

1. students first reflect and complete in writing one of the given sentence frames
2. then read their reflection to a partner
3. then the teacher selects a few reflections to be shared and recorded with the full group so that together the class builds a common understanding of the particular avenue of thinking.

The important takeaway for students from the math practice–focused reflection is what they learned about an avenue of thinking that they might use again in future problem solving. Leaving a math lesson knowing the answer to one problem is not nearly as helpful as leaving the lesson having gained a new insight into how to approach any number of math problems.

All five of our guiding principles come together in the end-of-routine math practice reflection as students do the cognitively demanding work (1) of thinking about their thinking. This multimodal (2), language-based (3) activity that places attention on learning to think mathematically helps students work from their learning strengths (4) to see mathematics as sensible and, more importantly, doable with effort (5).

> As you read about the routines in the next four chapters, think about the powerful understandings that get solidified and summarized for students during the math practice reflections.

Access Through Multiple Modalities and Multiple Representations

Woven throughout all the instructional routines in this book are opportunities for learners to engage with multiple mathematical representations and use multiple learning modalities. The mathematical practices call on students to make sense of, connect, model with, and use as tools a range of concrete and abstract mathematical representations. This offers multiple entry points for students with different processing strengths. In particular, it provides English language learners with a rich environment to develop language as they compare, consider, and connect the representations using gestures, annotations, and pointing to support the communication of their mathematical thinking. We've chosen multiple representations as an important element, because it is both an approach to supporting struggling learners that has been confirmed in the research and an important tool for helping students to meet various math practice goals. Each of the math practice routines in this book includes multiple representations for students to practice working with, using auditory (speaking and listening), visual (drawing and labeling), and physical (gesturing and moving around) approaches.

> As you read through the routines in this book, pause regularly to consider what representations and modalities are being used and how they support both access for special populations as well as math practice development for all students.

Math Practice–Focused Instructional Prompts

Because focusing on thinking—rather than answer-getting—may be unfamiliar for many students, math practice–focused instructional prompts are used regularly and with purpose throughout all our instructional routines. To illustrate what these prompts are and what's significant about students' responses to them, let's look at two contrasting examples using this problem:

> Together Evan, Katie, and McKenna had $865 when they left to go shopping. Evan spent $\frac{2}{5}$ of his money. Katie spent $40. McKenna spent twice as much as Evan. They each have the same amount of money left. How much money did each take shopping with them?

Mr. Wang's Class *(no math practice–focused prompts)*

When faced with a word problem, Mr. Wang often asks his students to identify the important information in the problem. In this problem, several students respond by saying "865 dollars," "Evan spent $\frac{2}{5}$," and "Katie spent $40." These students are focusing on and extracting the numbers provided in the problem and reading back bits of the problem statement. This is indeed important for solving the problem but falls short because it doesn't name the important quantities behind the numbers nor provide information about the relationships between those quantities. Some of his students say, "It's about Evan, Katie, and McKenna spending money," information about context that, again, is generally useful information but does not contribute much to determining a solution method.

Mrs. Paige's Class *(with a math practice–focused prompt)*

In Mrs. Paige's class, the math practice goal for today is related to MP2, so she is having her students focus not only on the quantities in the problem, but also what the problem tells them about how those quantities are related. She asks her students, "What are the important quantities in this problem? Are there other 'hidden' or implicit quantities in this problem that may not be explicitly stated?" and "How are those quantities related to each other?" This attention to quantities, and relationships between quantities, will help students say things like:

- "This problem is about the amount of money three different people took shopping, the number of dollars each spent, and the amount of money each had at the end."
- "Evan still has $\frac{3}{5}$ of the money he started with."
- "Because McKenna spent twice as much as Evan, she spent $\frac{4}{5}$ of the amount Evan started with. What she has left is the same as $\frac{3}{5}$ of Evan's money."
- "Katie's amount left is the same as $\frac{3}{5}$ of Evan's money."

Identifying these quantities and their relationships to each other helps students create a visual representation as part of the Comparing Quantities routine, and to use that visual to help them come up with a solution method. We'll say more about this in Chapter 3, but the key here is that the prompts to students are designed specifically to point attention to—and keep attention on—elements of the math practice, in this case "reasoning abstractly and quantitatively."

This is just one example, and there are different prompts specific to each routine that we'll point out. The specific math practice–focused prompts are intended to be used each time the routine is used, so that over time, the language becomes more familiar and the kinds of responses students should provide become more familiar to both you and your students. This language modeling can be especially helpful for English language learners, or students with language-based learning disabilities. The instructional routines and illustrative vignettes in subsequent chapters provide examples of instructional prompts worded to achieve a particular purpose, so as you read, keep in mind that the wording is specific and intentional.

> As you read through the routines in this book, pay attention to how students are prompted to talk about their thinking in terms of the specific math practices.

Four Essential Instructional Strategies in the Routines

In Chapter 1, we introduced guiding principles that characterize our approach to instruction that informs the design of the routines. The principles shaped our overall design of the routines and are ever-present in the background of all routines. In this chapter, we've now identified core elements that recur in different but recognizable ways across all the instructional routines in the following chapters that embody our guiding principles. The core elements describe the specific architecture of the routines; these parts of the routine are themselves part of the support for all students and are "baked in" to each routine. An awareness of both the principles and core elements provides you with context for the approach we take in all the routines. However, the most important parts of the routines for you to pay attention to are the essential instructional strategies that describe teacher and student actions that occur within the structure of the routine. These instructional strategies are the things that you actually do during the routine. They ensure that the routine does what it's intended to do, keeping a focus on the math thinking and providing access for a wide range of learners. They also support the overlapping best practices for special populations that we described in Chapter 1. They're customizable based on who your students are and what your thinking goal is. These strategies appear in each of the routines, though certain strategies will be more or less prominent in each. You can use them to your advantage, and we'll make suggestions for how to do so throughout the book.

- **Ask-yourself questions:** These questions embody the type of mathematical reasoning inherent in a particular math practice. Initially they are asked of students by the teacher, but eventually they are intended to become internalized by students as part of the way they think about a problem.

- **Annotation:** Teachers, and eventually students, annotate different representations in students' work to highlight a noticing related to or an important aspect of a particular avenue of thinking. Annotation also provides access by helping students connect math talk and gestures to visual representations.

- **Sentence frames and sentence starters:** These writing and speaking prompts are tailored in the routines to help teacher and students focus attention on a math practice and to provide support for language access and production.

- **The Four Rs—repeat, rephrase, reword, record:** There are key times in the routines when the teacher prompts students to repeat something they heard, then to rephrase it. The teacher often asks a different student to reword what was just said, then finally the teacher records it for the class. We'll say more about this strategy below.

In each routine, there are certain elements that are fixed, such as the sequence of steps or the focus of a final reflection on the use of a particular math practice, among others. However, there are also other key places in each routine where you have some choice about how you shape the routine to your students' needs. Chapter 7 provides some suggestions for using each practice, but as you gain familiarity with the routines, you will become better able to choose and modify them for your students.

As both you and your students gain comfort and familiarity with these four instructional strategies, you can use them throughout your mathematics lessons even when you are not focusing specifically on math practices. They will help you actively engage *all* your students as you teach them to think like mathematicians. In this section, we'll discuss what each strategy is, why it's used, and how its use is adapted to focus on the math practices.

Ask-Yourself Questions

Imagine we could look inside the minds of our students to see how they were thinking about a math problem. At the surface, we would likely see them thinking, *What's the answer?* If we could peel back that outermost layer of thinking, we might next be able to see what they had done to get an answer. In fact, if you ask most students to "explain their thinking," they will first provide you with a description of what they did, a list of the steps they followed, that often starts something like, "Well, first I did _____ and then I did _____."

If we were to peel back yet another layer to see the thinking underneath that list of steps, we might next learn about *why* they chose to take particular steps, *why* they did what they did. It's what we would hear if we prompted students to say, "Well, first I did _____ *because* _____." But to find the different avenues of thinking characterized by the math practices, we want to peel back one more layer to get at what's underneath why they did what they did. Buried under all those layers, there's some important thinking about what a student noticed mathematically about the problem when he or she was first getting started with it, what the student paid attention to in the mathematics of the problem, and what the student wondered about as he or she worked on the problem. This level of thinking mostly happens pretty invisibly inside a student's head and does not get recorded in any written work on the problem. This is the thinking we are trying to capture in the ask-yourself questions.

Some Sample Ask-Yourself Questions

Consider the following math problem:

A 20.5-gallon gas tank in a car is $\frac{4}{5}$ full.

How many more gallons will it take to fill the tank?

Take a moment to pay attention to these questions:

- How are you starting to think about this problem?
- What are you wondering?
- What questions are you asking yourself to make sense of the problem situation?

For example, perhaps you tackled the problem by seeing "$\frac{4}{5}$ full" and thinking about "$\frac{1}{5}$ empty" instead. You may have then thought of 20.5 as $20 + 0.5$ and found $\frac{1}{5}$ of each (4 and 0.1, respectively), and arrived at 4.1 gallons as the answer. If so, then you're like our friend Stephanie in Chapter 1 who reasons structurally. The kinds of ask-yourself questions that characterize your thinking might include:

- "How can I change the form of this number or expression to surface the underlying structure in the problem?"
- "How can I use mathematical properties to help me work on the problem?"

These ask-yourself questions may not have been questions you articulated to yourself quite in this way, but they capture the kind of thinking you were doing.

Or you may have approached the problem by taking a quick inventory of the important quantities in the problem, thinking "20.5 gallon tank . . . $\frac{4}{5}$ full . . . $\frac{1}{5}$ empty . . ." and picturing some kind of visual that helped you see the relationships between those quantities (Figure 2.1 shows one example of this).

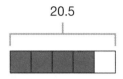

Figure 2.1

If so, you are like our friend Quinn in Chapter 1 who uses quantitative reasoning to make sense of the problem. The kinds of ask-yourself questions that characterize your thinking might include:

- "How can I represent this problem using diagrams or symbols?"

- "How can I represent the relationship so that I can see all the quantities, even those not explicitly stated in the problem?"

Or you may have approached the problem by starting to test different numbers to help you identify what steps you should use to solve it. For example, you could test possible answers of 10 gallons, 5 gallons, and 2 gallons to note what steps you were doing each time. It does not matter to this process that 10 gallons is a highly unlikely answer, because the focus is not on narrowing down the appropriate range of the possible answer (this is the goal of a "guess-and-check" strategy). Instead, the focus is on noticing what steps are repeated each time a number is tested (i.e., $5x = 20.5$) (Figure 2.2).

If so, you are like our friend Roberto who uses repeated reasoning to come to some generalizations. The kinds of ask-yourself questions that characterize your thinking might include:

- "Am I calculating the same way each time?"

- "How can I use the repetition to make my rule?"

Even though we may not explicitly articulate them, these kinds of questions drive our mathematical investigations. Making them explicit and using and reusing them with your students focus students' attention on a particular mathematical avenue of thinking, give the class a common language for talking about how you do that kind of thinking, and give

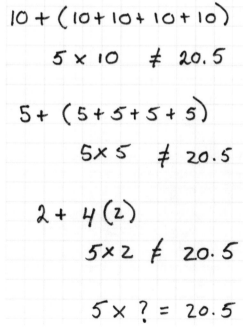

Figure 2.2

students general questions that they can internalize and use in other problem-solving situations. In Chapter 7, we provide a more complete list of ask-yourself questions for each avenue of thinking.

Teachers' Use of Ask-Yourself Questions

Ask-yourself questions can be a powerful instructional tool for you to use to get at the math practices in any mathematics lesson. Your goal is to teach your students how to ask these questions themselves when they are faced with an unfamiliar problem, but for them to learn to do so, they need to first see you model the use of these questions. The routines help you do that: specifically modeling their use (e.g., the teacher says, "When I see a word problem like this, I've learned to ask myself, how are the quantities related?"); reminding students to refer to the list of ask-yourself questions as thinking tools if they're stuck in a problem (e.g., the teacher says, "Remember, think like a mathematician and ask yourself, how are the quantities related?"); and generally prompting students to use these questions to guide their thinking (e.g., the teacher says, "What would be helpful to ask yourself given this type of problem?"). As you try out the various routines in this book, you will have the opportunity to choose which ask-yourself questions to highlight with your own students. Chapter 7 includes some specific examples of ask-yourself questions to use in each routine when you're first getting started; as you gain more familiarity with the routine, you can begin to choose or tailor your own ask-yourself questions.

Students' Use of Ask-Yourself Questions

The routines are also designed to help students pay attention to how their thinking connects to the various ask-yourself questions. Throughout the routines, students are prompted to ask themselves a specific question that reflects a particular math practice, such as *What can I count or measure in this situation?* (MP2), *How can I get the answer without doing all the calculations?* (MP7), *Am I counting the same way each time?* (MP8), and so on. Students are also asked throughout the routines to pay attention to what they are wondering, and the ask-yourself questions are provided to give them a language to describe the questions that implicitly underlie what they are wondering.

Ask-yourself questions can also be part of a useful problem-solving heuristic for students to use when they bump up against a nonroutine problem. Students with learning disabilities are frequently taught generic strategies to help them deal with unfamiliar, nonroutine problems (e.g., read, or reread, the question; circle the important numbers, and underline the keywords; choose a form, and write an equation; solve the problem, then check your answer). These generic problem-solving strategies can be a useful list of suggested steps for students to take; however, with this kind of strategy, the focus remains on procedures that move students toward an answer rather than on the student's thinking. In addition, the strategy only works if the student has familiarity with the problem type. Imagine instead a problem-solving heuristic that helps students focus on what they notice in the problem and links that to a set of ask-yourself questions. For example, the heuristic might look something like this:

1. Read the problem carefully.
2. Think about what you are noticing (i.e., quantities, structure, repetition).
3. Look at the lists of ask-yourself questions related to what you noticed.
4. Choose one or two questions that you think could help you enter this problem.
5. Answer that question or questions.
6. If the answer does not result in a viable solution strategy, repeat steps 2–5 with something else you noticed and another ask yourself question.

Instead of using a strategy that focuses on completing steps of a procedure, the ask-yourself questions can be part of a strategy that helps students select and then apply a viable avenue of mathematical thinking. As part of learning to regularly make use of the math practices in their reasoning, students are also learning to pay attention to how they think, and how to articulate it. The power in being able to do so is that once they can identify it and articulate it, it becomes a problem-solving tool they can use when stuck, to develop perseverance and grit.

Annotation

Annotation can help you draw students' attention to important connections or relationships in a problem. For example, the Connecting Representations routine in Chapter 4 prompts students to match two different types of representations (e.g., an algebraic expression and a written description of a rule, a bar diagram and a numerical equation, a graph and table). After one pair of students makes a match and the class discusses the connection, another pair of students annotates both representations so that all can more directly see the points of connection between the representations. Figure 2.3 shows an example of annotating a verbal description and graph to show how clues given in the text regarding the speed of the car (i.e., driving over the speed limit is fast, stopped means a zero speed, and continued more slowly indicates a rate slower than the "speeding" rate) can be seen in the graph as a distance–time relationship. The annotation—specifically the use of color, of different types of lines, and of words—helps students see the connections between the verbal description of the motion and the line segments showing three different distance–time relationships.

In this instance, students need to think structurally to relate the parts of the graph to the parts of the verbal description, so the annotation encourages the use of MP7. However, annotation can be used to support any of the math practices in which multiple representations are used, as you'll see throughout the subsequent chapters.

Ana drove from New York to Boston. She started by _driving over the speed limit_ and was _stopped_ by a police officer. Afterward, she _continued to Boston more slowly._

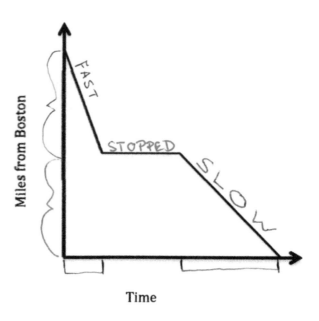

Figure 2.3

You can also use annotation to focus your students' attention on a mathematical process or on the mathematical characteristics of an image under discussion. For example, during the Recognizing Repetition routine in Chapter 5, annotation is used to highlight repetition in the counting, calculating, or constructing process that a student shares. Let's look at an example of this annotation from the following problem.

Crossing the River
(Driscoll 1999)

Eight adults and two children need to cross a river. A small boat is available that can hold one adult, one child, or two children. Everyone can row the boat. How many one-way trips does it take for all of them to cross the river? Describe how to work it out for two children and any number of adults.

In Figure 2.4, we see an example of how one student recorded the process she used to shuttle the adults and children across the river. As students named the repetition they saw in the shuttling process, the teacher used brackets to highlight the repeated steps and described the generalization of the repetition in words.

The Role of Annotation

Teachers using the routines in this book often start by modeling annotation for students. That modeling gives way to students having opportunities to annotate their own work and ultimately developing annotation as a tool they can choose to use when they see the need. The goal is for students to become comfortable enough with annotation that it becomes a routine way for them to make sense of the mathematics and communicate mathematically in the classroom. Though the process of annotation might be seen as an unnecessary step that takes time away from getting through the material of a lesson, it serves an important role. As students annotate their work, they get some additional processing time to make clearer in their own minds how the different representations in their work are related to each other. The visual elements of the annotation are especially helpful for English

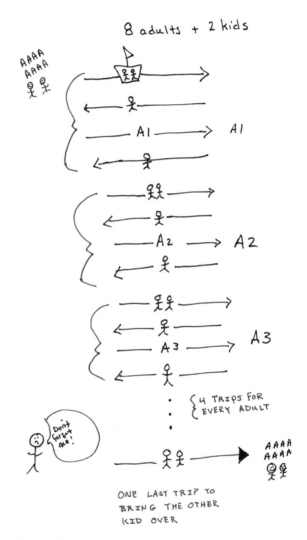

Figure 2.4

learners who may be struggling to understand and interpret the verbal explanations of their fellow students, or who can rely on it as an additional way to communicate their understanding. Annotation also creates a "residue of thinking" available for later reference, which is particularly helpful for students who struggle with attention and focus. And not only does it support those who might struggle in different ways, it also plays to the strengths of those students in your class who think visually.

Annotation also taps into several of the supporting math practices. Although it's easy to think of the "tools" in MP5, *use appropriate tools strategically*, as physical tools such as computers and calculators, annotation is a valuable tool that students can also choose to use strategically. Students can use annotation to make a more mathematically precise (MP6) and convincing argument (MP3).

Sentence Frames and Sentence Starters

The sentence starters and sentence frames used in these routines are intentionally worded to serve two purposes. First, they help students stay focused on the kind of mathematical thinking reflected by the math practice. They can also be used to focus partner work and whole-class discussion during a routine. For example, teachers might ask individual students to use a sentence starter when they share their thinking with a partner. ("I noticed _____" or "The difference between the two _____ is _____.") During partner work, to encourage focused discussion, the teacher might provide students with a sentence starter to use that says "I noticed _____. What did *you* pay attention to?" Or during whole-class discussion after a pair of students has explained their reasoning on a problem, a teacher might call on someone to rephrase the explanation using a sentence frame like "When this pair saw _____, it made them think _____." You've already seen an example of these kinds of sentence starters and sentence frames when we talked about using math practice–focused reflections, one of the core elements of the routines.

The second purpose sentence frames and sentence starters serve is to support those who struggle with language to collect and communicate their thoughts. They can serve as a powerful language development tool. A teacher can use them to target specific academic language—words, phrases, and sentence structures—crucial for developing the mathematics at hand. The descriptions of the routines and the accompanying vignettes in the book provide sample language frames, but you will want to think about how you would customize sentence starters and frames for your students in the particular lesson you are teaching.

The Four Rs: Repeat, Rephrase, Reword, Record

This essential strategy is an important one for helping students make sense of the classroom discussion that takes place throughout each of the routines. Building from our guiding principle that students learn best in a language-rich environment, these routines provide many opportunities for discourse. Therefore, it falls upon you to facilitate discussions with your students in each of the routines, and this strategy provides a structure for helping you to do so. When one of your students offers an idea during discussion, decide whether the student's idea relates to your thinking goal for the routine. If it does, and feels relevant to the discussion, that's where the Four Rs strategy comes into play:

The Four Rs Strategy	
Teacher Question and Decision Point	**Action to Take**
First, ask yourself: *Did all my students hear the idea?*	If not, then *repeat*: Call on a student to repeat what was said.
Next, ask yourself: *Did all my students understand the idea?*	If not, then *rephrase*: Call on one or two students to rephrase what was said. Rephrasing involves saying the idea again using different words. This provides additional processing time for those who need it, additional practice communicating for the speaker, and additional opportunity to make sense of the language for those students who need it.
Next, ask yourself: *Is now the time to press for precision in language?*	*If yes, then reword*: Say the idea again, substituting any mathematical or academic language that you want to have your students develop.
Finally, ask yourself: *What do I need to capture in the language and the thinking for reference by my students?*	*Record*: Publicly write down some record of the idea, using language you want students to use.

Figure 2.5

Of all the four essential strategies, this one requires the most in-the-moment decision making on your part. Sometimes, you may feel the need to use all four steps; other times, you may feel it's sufficient to just repeat, rephrase, and record. Other times, you may just repeat, rephrase, and reword and not have any need to record. You can use some or all the steps of this strategy as a template for facilitating mathematical discourse, depending on your goals for the discussion and the needs of your students. You'll see several different examples of part or all of this strategy in the vignettes in Chapters 3 through 6.

A Word About Recording

In these routines, *recording* simply refers to the documentation of important ideas that arise as part of the partner and whole-class discussions. Recording plays a vital role as a support for language. It supports productive, interpretive, and collaborative language.

Recording also plays a vital role as a memory support for those students who need it, capturing important ideas and language for later reference.

Research suggests that students effectively learn language when it's introduced as students need it, to support and develop their communication. This means not preteaching vocabulary as part of the routines, and instead recording keywords and phrases as the need arises during the routine.

The routines are also designed to help students build language authentically, so when you record, build from the students' own wording as a starting point. The options to rephrase and reword provide opportunities for you to help students refine their communication and incorporate any mathematical or academic language you want them to learn.

Familiarizing Yourself with the Routines

In the chapters that follow, we try to bring to life a specific instructional routine for each of the three mathematical avenues of thinking—reasoning abstractly and quantitatively, looking for and making use of structure, and looking for and expressing regularity in repeated reasoning—as well as the overarching MP1: *Make sense of problems and persevere in solving them.*

A "Backward" Approach?

You'll notice in the table of contents that we've chosen to talk first about the three avenues of thinking (Chapters 3–5) before we address "making sense of problems and persevering in solving them" in Chapter 6. Although this may seem out of order—after all, isn't making sense of a problem the first thing you need to do?—this order of chapters is intentional on our part. We'll make the case in Chapters 3, 4, and 5 that being able to use any of these three avenues of thinking is *precisely* how students can make sense of problems and persevere in solving them. But effectively making sense of a problem situation requires approaching it with a mathematician's eye, and that mathematician's eye gets developed along with the avenue of thinking as students learn what is mathematically important to pay attention to. Therefore, we invite you to bring your new understandings and images of the avenues of thinking to the familiar topic of problem solving addressed in Chapter 6.

Some General Recommendations

To best make use of the routines in the chapters that follow, we suggest the following steps for familiarizing yourself with each routine:

- **Get to know the purpose of the routine.** Each routine is designed to bring to the forefront some aspect of one of the math practices and to focus on thinking skills and ways of reasoning mathematically, regardless of the specific math task being used with it. Having that primary purpose of the routine clearly in mind will help you maintain a focus in your instruction on developing your students' ways of reasoning mathematically. Moreover, each routine does not necessarily address all aspects of the math practice; a routine may focus only on some part of the math practice. Be clear on what learning the routine helps your students gain.

- **Familiarize yourself with the core elements and essential strategies that are featured in the routine.** Each routine includes the core elements in slightly different ways and emphasizes particular essential strategies. The strategies that receive emphasis will be slightly different for each routine, so understanding which strategies get emphasis and how the core elements are used will help you develop a clear picture of the overall purpose and flow of the routine. For example, in Chapters 3 and 4, we highlight the use of sentence frames and starters and of annotation. In Chapters 5 and 6, we highlight the use of ask-yourself questions and the Four Rs. So although you may skip around Chapters 3–6 to try out different routines, we encourage you to read all four chapters to get the fullest picture of the purpose of these core elements and essential strategies.

- **Be sure to read through the vignette.** For each routine, we play out an illustration of the routine in use. You'll see this as a vignette with background commentary focused on either clarifying the flow of the routine, highlighting important teacher decision-making points, or ways in which the routine supports special populations in particular. Note that these vignettes capture an illustration of the routine's use once you and your students are somewhat familiar with the routine, so consider these as examples of your use of the routine on your fourth or fifth time through it. As with all new curricula or new instructional techniques, it takes a few times through them to fit them to your teaching style and understand the various parts.

- **Collect your questions about getting started and using the routine the first few times, then look ahead to Chapter 7 and the Appendices.** There are some general things to be said about the first time you use one of these routines that are pertinent across all routines. Then, there are some pieces of advice and guidance specific to each routine. You'll find this information in the final chapter of the book, so feel free to skip ahead to that chapter at whatever point in your reading you feel you need to. That chapter can easily be read in bits and pieces and is organized to try to address some key questions that we anticipate will arise. There are additional resources for Chapters 3–5 in the appendices that provide some specific math tasks. We believe that you don't need any new materials to implement the math practices well; you simply need to create a different "surround" around existing math tasks that you have from your materials. So we provide some sample tasks but also encourage you to look for math tasks from your own materials that could fit well with a particular routine.

- **In the vignette, note places where the teacher "delays instruction."** There are a number of places in the routines where you will see the teacher refraining from providing instruction to students where it might seem to you that he or she should be doing so. This happens particularly during individual think time or partner work in the routines. For example, at the start of the routines when students have individual think time, as you circulate, you may see students who are building a pattern with manipulatives or working on a written problem in a way that does not appear to be correct. The teacher does not intervene to correct the student or to provide explanation about how to do it (although explanations to clarify the task are of course appropriate!). This is because both individual think time and partner work are important opportunities for students to develop and explore their own thinking as well as that of their partners. The routines are designed to give students multiple opportunities to develop and practice aspects of the avenues of thinking. False starts and dead ends are a natural part of that development, providing contrast so the student can be more productive the next time around.

The routines give you a structure that has been intentionally designed—and used in many classrooms already—to focus your students' learning on these important avenues of thinking so that you can free up your own brain space to work creatively with the ways in which your own students are developing these avenues of thinking. Enjoy trying them out and making them your own!

Capturing Quantities

An Instructional Routine to Support Students
Reasoning Abstractly and Quantitatively

Mrs. Quaid sat down in the teacher's room and began going over a stack of
homework papers. The students were doing fine on the fractions skills practice,
but when they got to the word problems, it was a different story. They would read
the problem; highlight the numbers, keywords, and question; and then stop. She
looked at Charlie's paper (Figure 3.1). *He at least had tried to solve the problem. But
he got the wrong answer. What did he do?* she wondered.

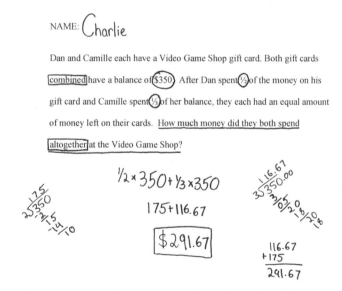

NAME: Charlie

Dan and Camille each have a Video Game Shop gift card. Both gift cards
combined have a balance of $350. After Dan spent ½ of the money on his
gift card and Camille spent ⅓ of her balance, they each had an equal amount
of money left on their cards. How much money did they both spend
altogether at the Video Game Shop?

$$\tfrac{1}{2} \times 350 + \tfrac{1}{3} \times 350$$

$$175 + 116.67$$

$$\boxed{\$291.67}$$

$$\begin{array}{r} 116.67 \\ +175 \\ \hline 291.67 \end{array}$$

Figure 3.1

Charlie had clearly read the problem carefully, circling the numbers, boxing key-
words, and underlining the question. But then what? The 350 was the total amount
of money on both cards together, not the amount on each of their individual cards.

It looked as though Charlie saw the $\frac{1}{2}$ and $\frac{1}{3}$, and because 350 was the only other number in the problem, he took a half and a third of that. Then he added because he saw *combined* and *altogether* and thought about addition.

Charlie was not the only student with the answer $291.67. Several other students, who had also circled the numbers and boxed *combined* and *altogether*, had also gotten the same wrong answer.

What Charlie and the other students did is common; they relied on the strategy of highlighting numbers and looking for keywords, and only read the problem superficially. As a result, they jumped to an incorrect calculation without considering the quantities and relationships beneath the numbers and keywords. Although this strategy can be a useful place to start for many students, it omits a critical part of making sense of the problem that sits squarely in the "quantitative" avenue of thinking: getting students to move beyond circling numbers and boxing keywords and begin to consider the quantities and relationships in a math problem.

When mathematical thinkers approach a problem by reasoning abstractly and quantitatively, they pause to pay attention to all of the quantities in the problem situation and explore the relationships between them. Like Mrs. Quaid's students, they look at numbers in a problem statement, but they don't stop there. They ask themselves if the number communicates a value of a quantity (e.g., the $350 in the problem at the start of the chapter is the value for the total amount on both gift cards combined) or if it describes a relationship between two quantities (e.g., the $\frac{1}{2}$ is describing a relationship between the amount of money Dan spent and the total amount of money that was on his card to start).

In this chapter, we'll explore what it means for students to reason abstractly and quantitatively and introduce the instructional routine *Capturing Quantities* to support all students' development of this avenue of thinking.

What Does It Mean to "Reason Abstractly and Quantitatively"?

In Chapter 1, Quinn's thinking provided a glimpse of one student's abstract and quantitative reasoning. Let's look more deeply at what characterizes that kind of thinking.

Identifying Quantities

For starters, let's look at what a *quantity* is, and how it differs from a number or value. When we talk about quantities in mathematics, we are referring to things that can be counted or measured; things that could be assigned a numeric value or variable. A quantity has three components: its value, its label, and its sign (positive or negative). We can describe quantities by using the phrase starter "The number of _____" or "The amount of _____." For example, what are the quantities in this scenario?

> Each year, Quinn plants 24 flowers in his garden. This year, he planted only red flowers and purple flowers. Quinn prefers purple, so he planted twice as many purple flowers as red flowers.

A problem stem is a word problem in which the question has been removed, so that there is no specific question to answer. Providing only the problem stem encourages students to consider quantities and relationships. The stem can be followed by any one of a number of questions that form different math problems.

Most people readily answer "24." Although 24 does refer to the value of one of the quantities in this situation, 24 is a number. The quantity that 24 refers to is the total number of flowers in the garden. What are other quantities in the scenario? Take a minute to list as many quantities as you are able. Ask yourself, *What can I count or measure in this problem situation?*

Additional quantities referred to in the scenario include:

- the number of red flowers
- the number of purple flowers
- the number of colors of flowers planted.

So it's important to distinguish between the quantities in the problem, the value of each of those quantities, and the numbers provided in the problem. Sometimes, a number is given in the problem as a value for one of the quantities, sometimes it's not (see Figure 3.2).

Quantities Listed in the Problem	The Value of the Quantity	Numbers Listed in the Problem
The total number of flowers planted	24	24
The number of red flowers	Not yet known	No number listed
The number of purple flowers	Not yet known	No number listed
The number of colors of flowers planted	2	Not listed

Figure 3.2

We know the value for only one of these additional quantities, the number of colors of flowers planted, 2. Although we may not know the value for other quantities, they may be quantities that we will represent with variables. In fact, articulating the quantities in a problem situation is a first step to writing equations and expressions, and a crucial step as the problem situations become more complex. Asking students to think about what can be counted or measured in a problem situation and providing the phrase starters "the number of _____" and "the amount of _____" are good first steps.

A Note About Greater Precision in Language

When we talk about quantities with students, it's typical to use an easy label for a quantity such as "the red flowers" or "the purple flowers." However, with more precise use of language, you can support students' development of quantitative reasoning. Consider always carefully describing quantities with language that points to amounts and values. For example, instead of saying "red flowers" or "purple flowers," say *the number of* red flowers" or "*the number of* purple flowers."

This is an opportunity to model the use of precision (MP6) in your own language and to encourage it in your students. It will also help make clearer to all students what this quantity refers to, as there will often be more than one quantity related to a particular thing in a problem. Take for example "Dan's gift card" from the task at the beginning of this chapter. Quantities related to Dan's card include the amount of money on Dan's card to start, the amount of money remaining on Dan's card after he spent half, and the amount of gift card money he spent. Using the label "Dan's gift card" is ambiguous; with more precise use of language, you can highlight these quantities and avoid this ambiguity.

Describing Relationships Between Quantities

A relationship describes a mathematical connection between two or more quantities. A mathematical relationship includes the quantities that are in the relationship as well as the way in which they are related. What relationships were described in the problem situation?

- "He planted twice as many purple flowers as red flowers." This means that the number of purple flowers *is two times* the number of red flowers.
- The number of red flowers combined with the number of purple flowers *is the same as* the total number of flowers.

If we interpret these relationships, we may be able to describe them in additional ways that may uncover further meaning.

- The number of red flowers *is half of* the number of purple flowers.

One of the steps of the Four Rs strategy is especially relevant in this routine. Rephrasing a relationship is particularly powerful because it provides different equivalent ways to see the relationship and thus helps students avoid mistakes when they represent the relationship abstractly. For example, it is not uncommon for students to incorrectly represent "he planted twice as many purple flowers as red flowers" as $2P = R$, where P is the number of purple flowers and R is the number of red flowers. This common mistake results from directly translating words into symbols as you read left to right, rather than reasoning about the relationship described.

Rephrasing "he planted twice as many purple flowers as red flowers" to "the number of red flowers is half the number of purple flowers" can both reinforce students' understanding of the inverse relationship between "twice as many" and "half the number of" and provides a phrase that is easier to accurately represent symbolically.

Representing Quantities and Relationships

After listing the quantities and relationships, the next step to reasoning abstractly and quantitatively is to represent them in a way that elicits deeper meaning. Teachers have always encouraged their students to draw a picture as a helpful problem-solving technique. But sometimes, those pictures are representations of some of the items in the problem or some kind of visual representation of the solution. The kinds of diagrams we're describing here are particularly powerful as thinking tools for students, because they are a "picture" of the quantities in the problem and how those quantities are related. It is a picture of the abstract relationships that exist in the problem. (For more on using diagrams as thinking tools, see Driscoll, Nikula, and DePiper [2016].) For example, one way to represent the problem situation describing Quinn's garden is in a diagram—the type shown in Figure 3.3 is often referred to as a bar, tape, or strip diagram.

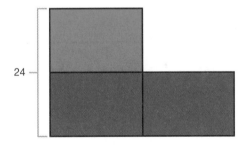

Figure 3.3

What relationships between the quantities are represented in the diagram in Figure 3.3? Take a minute to describe all of the relationships that you see.

Did your list include either or both of the following?

- The number of red flowers is $\frac{1}{2}$ the number of purple flowers.
- The ratio of purple flowers to red flowers is 2 to 1.

As you interpret this diagram, notice that there is an implicit quantity that becomes visible: the difference between the number of red and the number of purple flowers. That implied quantity may show up in different ways in the visual representation depending on how you're thinking about the implied quantity. For example, you may see this implied quantity in the "empty space" to the right of the red flower bar (Figure 3.4) and

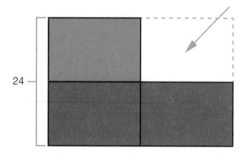

24 —

Figure 3.4

think of this quantity as the number of additional red flowers Quinn would need to plant in his garden if he wanted to have an equal number of each type of flower. Developing the capacity to see implied quantities when interpreting problem situations will help build students' facility with reasoning abstractly and quantitatively.

Now that we have a visual model of the quantities and relationships stated in the problem situation, we are able to uncover relationships that were not explicitly stated in the problem situation. We refer to these as "hidden relationships." Take a minute to connect the following hidden relationships to the diagram above:

- The number of red flowers is $\frac{1}{3}$ of the total number of flowers.
- The number of purple flowers is $\frac{2}{3}$ of the total number of flowers.

It turns out that these implied quantities and hidden relationships that often surface while interpreting a diagram can be very useful in answering the question that accompanies the problem stem. The bulleted list below provides a number of different possibilities for the question that could accompany our original problem stem, any one of which could be answered more easily with the use of the diagram.

> Problem Stem: Each year, Quinn plants 24 flowers in his garden. This year, he planted only red flowers and purple flowers. Quinn prefers purple, so he planted twice as many purple flowers as red flowers.

The following questions could be posed from this problem stem:

- How many red flowers did Quinn plant?
- How many purple flowers did Quinn plant?
- How many more purple flowers than red flowers did Quinn plant?
- What fraction/percent of his total flowers are purple? Are red?

Abstracting Problem Situations

Identifying the important quantities and relationships in a problem situation is a crucial part of making sense of a problem, but to solve the problem students must be able to represent those quantities and relationships abstractly using numeric expressions, diagrams, tables, algebraic equations, and so on, and then manipulate those representations without necessarily thinking about what they represent in the context. Figure 3.5 provides exam-

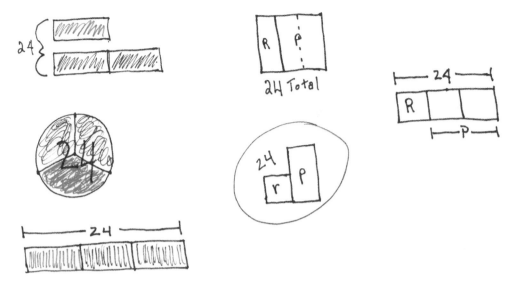

Figure 3.5

ples of diagrams that capture quantities and relationships. The Common Core Standards for Mathematical Practice refer to this as "decontextualizing."

It is equally important for students to be able to do the inverse—to be able to "contextualize." When students contextualize, they connect the mathematical work they've done back to the problem context.

The capacity to move back and forth between a context and an abstract mathematical representation of the context—to contextualize and decontextualize—is a hallmark of reasoning abstractly and quantitatively (MP2).

Let's look at an example from grade 8. The Quinn's Garden problem stem might be followed by the prompt: "Write a system of equations that represents the situation, and use it to find out how many red flowers Quinn planted." When faced with a task like this, many students struggle to define their variables or to set up their equations. However, we can look at "defining their variables" as identifying the important unknown quantities in the situation (e.g., the number of red flowers and the number of purple flowers) and "setting up equations" as representing the relationships between those quantities algebraically. So creating a diagram of the quantities and relationships becomes a strategy for solving the problem. The work might look like that shown in Figure 3.6.

So, developing the capacity to identify and represent quantities and relationships provides an entry point to abstracting the problem situation with variables and equations, where variables and expressions represent unknown quantities and equations represent relationships. Without this capacity to reason quantitatively and abstractly, students are often left to pull numbers from the problem and begin calculating based on keywords

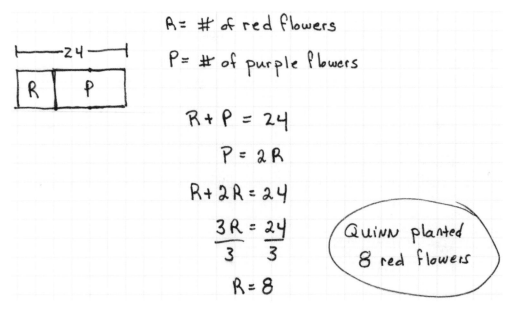

$$A = \text{\# of red flowers}$$
$$P = \text{\# of purple flowers}$$

$$R + P = 24$$
$$P = 2R$$
$$R + 2R = 24$$
$$\frac{3R}{3} = \frac{24}{3}$$
$$R = 8$$

Quinn planted 8 red flowers

Figure 3.6

or translate words into algebraic notation literally, reading from left to right without any understanding of the relationships of the numbers to each other.

An Overview of the Capturing Quantities Routine

The Capturing Quantities instructional routine is designed to focus students' attention on the quantities lurking behind the numbers and on the relationships between them.

The Steps of the Routine

The Capturing Quantities routine has five parts to it. Recall from Chapter 2 that each routine begins with an initial introduction to the routine (Part 1), including sharing a mathematical thinking goal with your students, and ends with a student reflection on how they developed their mathematical thinking and how they might use it in future problems (Part 5).

Parts 2, 3, and 4 are unique to this routine. In the Capturing Quantities routine, students read a problem stem that refers to multiple quantities and at least one relationship. Students articulate the quantities and relationships referred to in the problem stem (Part 2) and represent them visually by creating diagrams (Part 3). They discuss the diagrams, uncovering a deeper understanding of the problem situation and/or a solution path (Part 4).

These next sections provide a brief overview of the five parts of the routine. Later on, we provide a classroom illustration of what this routine looks like in action, and we'll highlight particular supports for special populations.

Part 1: *Launch the Routine*

When launching the routine, the teacher identifies the thinking goal for the routine and reviews the steps of the routine. It is critical that students understand that they are "capturing quantities" to develop the habit of looking for quantities and relationships in math problems. That is, they are not working on this activity to get the answer to this one particular problem, but rather to develop a way of thinking mathematically that will help them find answers to any number of problems.

Steps for Part 1

1. Display and explain the thinking goal. For example, you might say, "Today we are going to learn how to think like mathematicians. We are going to learn how to look for the quantities and relationships behind the numbers in a problem statement." (See Chapter 7 for examples of thinking goals you can use with this routine.)

2. Display and explain the flow and format of the routine. Help students understand that they will be identifying quantities and relationships individually, then sharing their thinking with a partner and discussing in the full group; creating diagrams to represent those relationships first individually, then with a partner; discussing each other's diagrams in the full group; and finally, reflecting on their learning.

Part 2: *Identify Quantities and Relationships*

In the second part of the Capturing Quantities routine, the focus is on learning to read for quantities and relationships. Using a think-pair-share structure, students interpret a problem stem and identify and discuss quantities and their relationships. The teacher provides an ask-yourself question and individual think time. Students share quantities and relationships with each other, then in the whole class as the teacher helps students reword and record their thinking through specific annotation.

Removing the question from a word problem is critical to the use of this routine—at least for the first several times you use it—because it prohibits students' tendency to immediately begin trying to solve the problem without first making sense of the problem situation. At the end of the routine, you can provide a question for your students to answer from the problem stem. As your students gain familiarity with looking for quantities and relationships in a problem, you can move away from using problem stems, and students will start to focus on quantities and relationships more habitually with "regular" problems that do pose a question.

Steps for Part 2

Individual Think Time

1. Read the problem situation together, and help students identify the important quantities and relationships in the problem stem. Help students focus on the quantities by having them ask themselves, *What can I count or measure in this situation?*

Pair

2. Have students share the quantities and relationships they identified with a partner.

Share

3. First elicit and record important quantities in the full group. Provide starters to focus attention on quantities and provide language support:

   The number of _____.

   The amount of _____.

4. Then have students share and rephrase relationships between the quantities. Record relationships, including alternative wording of key relationships. Use the frame to provide focus and language support:

   (Quantity *A*) is (related in this way) to (Quantity *B*).

Part 3: Create Diagrams

In this next part of the instructional routine, the focus is on helping students create a visual representation of the quantities and relationships they have identified, and to think more about how the quantities are related. They begin to think about a representation on their own, then refine their thinking with a partner. Together, partners create a diagram that they think best captures the quantities and relationships. Ask-yourself questions like "How much bigger/smaller is one quantity than another?" and "How can I show how much bigger/smaller one quantity is in my diagram?" help students articulate and represent relationships more precisely.

Steps for Part 3

Individual Think Time

1. Provide students individual think time to begin representing the important quantities and relationships in a diagram. Keep the time short—enough time for students to generate some ideas and begin generating a diagram, but not so much that they have created a complete diagram. This time lets students get ready to discuss their ideas about how to represent the quantities and relationships in a diagram.

Pair

2. Have students share how they started to represent the quantities and relationships. Provide starters and frames like the following to support sharing:

    How did you represent _____?

    I showed _____ by _____.

3. After students share their initial ideas, have them work together to create a diagram that they think best represents all the important quantities and relationships in the problem statement.

While partners work:

- circulate and observe the variety of diagrams in the room. Look for those created by more than one pair, those that represent quantities but not all the relationships, and those that uncover an unstated relationship

- consider how you will select and sequence the diagrams (approximately three) for the full-group discussion.

4. When you've identified a diagram to be analyzed by the full group, have the students who created it re-create the diagram on chart paper or on the board.

> NOTE: Ask them to re-create the diagram so that it only includes the values for quantities explicitly given in the problem situation, omitting any other contextual referents, labels, and/or calculations. (See Figures 3.7 and 3.8.) The class will use the unlabeled diagram to analyze and discuss quantities and relationships and then connect it to components of the context or word problem. Posting a labeled diagram leaves little to discuss. (In the next step of the routine, the class will discuss the diagram and add labels and annotation together.)

Figure 3.7 Original student diagram   **Figure 3.8** Re-created unlabeled diagram

Part 4: *Discuss Diagrams*

Finally, students have an opportunity to practice making sense of an unlabeled, unfamiliar diagram by looking for quantities and relationships. This helps students develop an eye for features of visuals that hold mathematical meaning and surface hidden relationships and implied quantities in a problem statement.

During this part of the routine, post one of the diagrams from Part 3 (unlabeled), give students a few seconds of individual think time to make sense of the diagram, and then have them talk with a partner about where they see the quantities and relationships represented. Students share their observations in the full group and the teacher annotates the diagram to highlight quantities and relationships.

Steps for Part 4

Individual Think Time

1. Select and post a student pair's unlabeled diagram. Give students a few seconds of individual think time to interpret the representation. Ask questions like, "What quantities can you identify?" and "What relationships do you notice?"

Pair

2. Prompt students to talk with a partner about where and how they see the quantities and relationships represented in the diagram.

Share and Discuss

3. Ask one or two students who did not create the diagram to discuss features of the diagram that clued them into quantities and relationships from the problem situation. When possible, press students to notice or name quantities and relationships not explicitly stated in the problem but that are now visible in the visual representation.

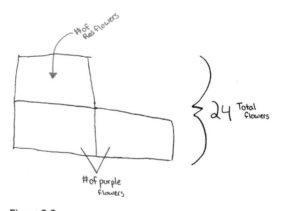

Figure 3.9

4. Annotate. As students share, annotate the diagram to highlight where and how students are identifying quantities and relationships in the diagram. (See Figure 3.9 as an example.)

Part 5: *Reflect on Quantitative Thinking*

In the last part of the routine, students reflect on what they have learned about reasoning quantitatively that will help them in their future problem solving and math learning. This final and critical component of the Capturing Quantities routine is where students solidify their learning. If time is running short, it is better to discuss fewer diagrams and save time for the reflection than to skip or shortchange this opportunity to reflect on the avenue of thinking.

Steps for Part 5

Individual Write Time

1. Frame the reflection by revisiting the thinking goal for this routine. Provide students with sentence starters and frames to focus their reflection (e.g., "When looking for quantities in a word problem, I learned to _____." or "When analyzing a diagram I learned to pay attention to _____ because _____."). Give students 1–3 minutes of quiet writing time to reflect and complete a sentence frame.

Pair

2. Have students share what they wrote with a partner. Listen in as partners share, and select two or three ideas related to the thinking goal to be shared in the full group.

Share

3. Have two or three students share what they learned about identifying, surfacing, and representing quantities and relationships. Record the statements and post for future reference.

The entire routine-at-a-glance is shown in Figure 3.10 (on the next page). As you look at the routines across these chapters, note the parallels between the flow of each routine; this can help you become familiar with them more easily.

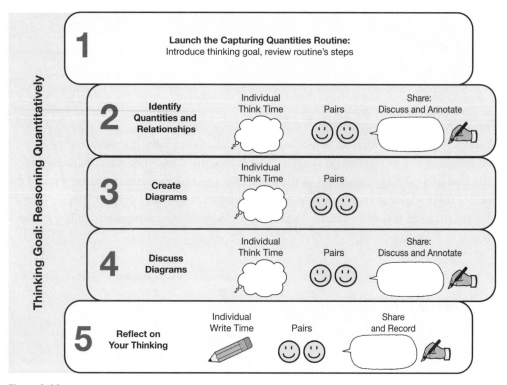

Figure 3.10

Essential Strategies in the Routine

Although all the essential strategies are involved in this routine, the essential strategies of annotation and sentence frames and starters are particularly crucial for providing focus and access in this routine.

Essential Strategies

- Ask-yourself questions
- **Annotation**
- **Sentence frames and sentence starters**
- Four Rs: repeat, rephrase, reword, record

Annotation

This essential strategy gets special attention in this routine because it is critical to helping students make sense of the diagrams that represent the quantities and relationships. Annotation involves adding shading, color, dotted lines, words, labels, and so on—anything that will help highlight and make explicit for students how the quantities and relationships appear in the diagram. Look for the use of annotation in particular in:

- Part 2 when the whole class lists ideas for quantities and relationships in the problem stem

- Part 4 when the whole class analyzes diagrams to see how they illustrate the quantities and the relationships between them.

Sentence Frames and Sentence Starters

The sentence frames and sentence starters in this routine are specifically designed to focus students' attention on quantities and relationships, rather than simply on numbers and keywords, and to model language for students to use in talking about these quantities and relationships. Sentence starters like "The number of _____," combined with ask-yourself questions such as "What can you count in this situation?" help students move beyond the numbers given in a problem to the quantities those numbers enumerate. Once students have identified important quantities in a problem situation, the next step is to articulate how those quantities are related. A sentence frame like "The number of _____ is _____ the number of _____" helps students move from simply looking for "clue words" to actually thinking about and describing a relationship between quantities when answering questions like "How are the quantities related?" and "How can I describe the relationship in another way?"

Look for the use of sentence frames and starters in particular in

- Part 2, when students first share and discuss the quantities and relationships they notice in the problem

- Part 3, when pairs talk with each other about how they are working on creating a diagram

- Part 4, when the whole class works together to annotate diagrams.

Challenges, Opportunities, and Supports for Students with Specific Needs

Two hallmarks of the "quantitative" avenue of thinking are the capacity to contextualize and decontextualize and the ability to identify and represent quantities and relationships with visuals. Both provide valuable opportunities for special populations.

Students with Learning Disabilities

The quantitative avenue of thinking calls on students to contextualize and decontextualize, moving back and forth seamlessly between the tangible context of the problem and abstract mathematical notation and representations. For many students who have conceptual processing difficulties, decontextualizing is a tall order. To support these students, the Capturing Quantities routine uses diagrams as a representational middle step toward abstraction. The diagrams help students to "see" quantities and the relative sizes between them described by the given relationships. As the teacher and students together discuss the diagrams, the teacher annotates the features being discussed, helping students connect the verbal to the visual. This builds visual-spatial processing ability; those students for whom it is a weakness get additional experience, and other students leverage it as a learning strength.

Supporting Students with Learning Disabilities When Using This Routine

- Consistently provide the individual think time throughout the routine.
- Help students identify what each part of the diagram means in relation to the context of the problem.
- Use annotation (color, shading, labels, and so on) to help clarify what each part of the diagram represents in the problem.
- Use sentence frames and sentence starters to provide consistent language as you talk about the different quantities and relationships.
- Choose contexts that are familiar to your students.
- Build on the familiarity students have with searching for numbers and keywords in the problem to help them see what quantity or relationships the number might be describing.

English Language Learners

The Capturing Quantities routine places a premium on language, as it is through language that quantitative and abstract reasoning is developed. Students develop increasing precision in the language they use to describe quantities as they gradually learn to identify quantities as something that can be counted or measured. Some sentence starters are used to support this greater precision in language when identifying quantities in a problem, such as "I can count the number of _____" and "I can measure the amount of _____." Other starters are used to name quantities, such as "the number of _____" and "the amount of _____." This helps transition English language learners (ELLs) beyond single-word labels (e.g., *flowers*) to phrases more precisely describing quantities (e.g., *the total number of flowers*). The sentence starters are posted, referenced, and used throughout the routine as students develop and communicate about their quantitative reasoning in pairs and during whole-class discussions.

Once students have identified the quantities, describing the relationships between quantities also provides fertile ground for language production as relationships are stated, repeated, and rephrased throughout the routine.

Providing students with a mathematical comparison frame such as "(Quantity A) is (relationship to) (Quantity B)" supports sentence-level language production and is critical to describing a mathematical relationship precisely. For example, a comparison statement like "The number of purple flowers is twice the number of red flowers" provides a range of options for language development:

- If your ELLs need practice speaking, record the comparison statement when it is made, and have students read and repeat the statement.

- If you want your ELLs to work on describing quantities verbally, provide a sentence frame like "The number of _____ is twice the number of _____" or "_____ is twice _____."

- If you want ELLs to work on the comparison language that describes the relationship, omit that piece of the frame, for example: "The number of purple flowers is _____ the number of red flowers" or "The number of red flowers is _____ the number of purple flowers."

- If your ELLs are ready to pull it all together, provide the overarching sentence structure "(Quantity A) is (relationship to) (Quantity B)" and a list of quantities (e.g., the number of purple flowers, the number of red flowers, the total number of flowers, etc.) and a list of descriptors (e.g., twice, two times, twice as much, double, half, and so on).

Whatever your language goal, the routine provides multiple passes at language as students cycle in and out of partner and full-group discussions. In addition, multiple experiences with the routine compound the practice opportunities.

Supporting English Language Learners When Using This Routine

- Use phrase starters, sentence starters, and sentence frames to help students communicate their quantitative reasoning.

- Repeat, rephrase, reword, and record quantities and relationships to help students access and produce academic language.

- Use visual cues such as gestures and annotation (e.g., color, shading, labels, and so on) to help students connect spoken language to mathematical ideas within the diagrams.

- Prompt students to use partner time to practice saying ideas they will share in the full group.

Capturing Quantities in Action

The following vignette provides an illustration of the Capturing Quantities routine, focusing on excerpts at key points where there are supports for students with learning disabilities as well as supports for ELLs.

To focus on these supports, the vignette portrays a classroom that is already starting to be familiar with the routine. This is the fourth time the students have used the routine, so they now understand the flow of the routine and the nature of quantities and relationships. They also understand that a diagram represents quantities and mathematical relationships. (For more information on how to first introduce the routine to students, see Chapter 7. For additional suggestions for math tasks to use in this routine, see Appendix C.)

Classroom Snapshot: Ms. Quaid's Sixth-Grade Math Class

Ms. Quaid's class includes two students with an Individualized Education Program (IEP) and two English learners.

- Maria and Sam have IEPs:
  - Maria is a concrete thinker who sticks close to the numbers and story in a math word problem. She is comfortable with numbers and performing memorized procedures. She likes to draw and has neat and organized notes.
  - Sam struggles with attention and organization. He can perseverate on a particular detail and have trouble shifting attention. Inferences are hard for Sam to make. He is skilled with numbers and computation and can manipulate numbers easily in his head.

- Hoang and Nguyen are the ELLs.
  - Assessment results and observations indicate Hoang is a level 3 based on the WIDA (World-class Instructional Design and Assessment) descriptions of English language proficiency. Vietnamese is spoken at home.
  - Nguyen's family moved into the district when she was in first grade. This year, she was assessed at an English language development proficiency level 5. Vietnamese is spoken at home.

Mrs. Quaid wrote the Video Game Shop task after overhearing Sam talking with some classmates about a new video game he bought with a gift card he had received for his birthday. Mrs. Quaid thought using a familiar context would help Sam access the math, as he typically struggles to make sense of word problems, and she knew that having a relevant context would also support other students.

PART 1: LAUNCH

Mrs. Quaid launches the Capturing Quantities routine by briefly revisiting the purpose and flow of the routine, and she introduces her thinking goal for the lesson: "Today we're learning how to find quantities and relationships in word problems and diagrams."

PART 2: IDENTIFY QUANTITIES AND RELATIONSHIPS

In this part of the routine, students practice identifying quantities and relationships. Notice the use of a problem stem, with no question to answer; this helps students focus on the quantities, rather than on finding the right answer.

Mrs. Quaid projects the problem stem and invites a student to read it aloud. (A set of sample PowerPoint slides for the full routine can be found in Appendix B.)

> **Dan and Camille each have a Video Game Shop card. Both cards combined have a balance of $350. After Dan spent $\frac{1}{2}$ of the money on his card and Camille spent $\frac{1}{3}$ of her balance, they each had an equal amount of money left on their cards.**

Note to readers: Take a moment to think about the important information and sketch a diagram that represents the important information yourself before reading further.

Individual Think Time and Pairs

Mrs. Quaid asks one of her students to read the problem stem aloud to the class, then directs students to spend one minute of silent individual thinking time to identify the important information in the problem situation. She uses the ask-yourself question "What can I count or measure?" as a prompt for students to look for quantities during this think time. While students are working silently, she sets up columns labeled "The number of . . . " and "The amount of . . . " on chart paper in anticipation of students sharing out.

After one minute, Mrs. Quaid directs students to talk with a partner for two minutes to share what they identified as important information in the problem. As they talk, Mrs. Quaid circulates and listens in on student conversations to hear what they are identifying as quantities and relationships between those quantities.

Share and Discuss (•)

Mrs. Quaid (*Bringing the whole class together*): Let's create a list of the important information. What are the important quantities in this problem stem? (*Pointing to the phrase starters that she wrote on the chart paper*) I'd like you to use the starter, "the number of _____" or "the amount of _____." OK, Maria?

Maria: 350.

Mrs. Quaid (*Acknowledging Maria's response, but redirecting*): OK, so you see the number 350. What is the *quantity* that has a value of 350? (*Pointing to the phrase starter*) What is 350 the number of?

Maria: Dollars. 350 dollars.

Mrs. Quaid: And what quantity does 350 dollars refer to? (*Pointing to the phrase starters*) The number or amount of what?

Maria: The amount of money on both gift cards.

Mrs. Quaid: And is this before or after they've spent any of it?

Maria: Before Dan and Camille buy video games.

Mrs. Quaid (*Modeling the language*): So the quantity is the total amount of money on both gift cards to start. And the value of that quantity is $350. (••) (*She records "total amount of money on both gift cards to start [$350]" on chart paper.*) [See Figure 3.11.] So one strategy for finding a quantity in a word problem is to look for a number like Maria did, and then ask yourself, "What quantity does that number represent?"

(•) The purpose of the discussion at this point in the routine is to help students generate a class list of the important quantities and the relationships between them, both modeling the process of identifying them as well as modeling the language you use to talk about them.

(••) Note that Mrs. Quaid is building on Maria's familiarity with noticing a number in the problem statement. She uses the phrase starters "the number of _____" and "the amount of _____" to help Maria connect the number to the underlying quantity it represents. Mrs. Quaid ends by describing Maria's attention to numbers as the first step of a strategy for identifying quantities.

Mrs. Quaid: What are other quantities in this problem stem? (*Students identi-fy a variety of quantities as Mrs. Quaid records them.*)

Quantities

The amount of . . .	The number of . . .
Total amount of money on both gift cards to start ($350)	# of dollars Dan spent
Amt. of money on Dan's card to start	# of dollars Camille spent
Amt. of money on Camille's card to start	# of dollars Dan has left
Amt. of money Camille had left	

Figure 3.11

Now that the class has a list of quantities, Mrs. Quaid turns the discussion to the relationships between the quantities.

Mrs. Quaid: What do we know about how these quantities are related to each other?

Gloria: The amount of money Dan spent is $\frac{1}{2}$ the amount he started with.

Mrs. Quaid: Which two quantities are related in that statement—the amount of money Dan spent is $\frac{1}{2}$ the amount he started with?

Gloria: The number of dollars Dan spent (*Mrs. Quaid points to this phrase in the list*) and the amount of money on Dan's card to start. (*Mrs. Quaid points again, then records it.*) [See Figure 3.12.]

Mrs. Quaid: What is another relationship that is described in the problem stem?

Charlie: They have the same amount of money at the end.

Mrs. Quaid: So, what are the two quantities that are the same or equivalent (*Points to the list of quantities*)?

Charlie: Oh (*Reading from the list*), the amount of money Camille had left and the number of dollars Dan has left. (*Mrs. Quaid records*) [See Figure 3.12.]

Mrs. Quaid: Are we good? Have we identified all the quantities that are related? Kerry?

Kerry: No. We know $\frac{1}{3}$, we know, um, we know the amount of money on Ca-mille's card is $\frac{1}{3}$. No, wait, we know (*Pauses*) the amount of money (*Pauses*) Camille spent is $\frac{1}{3}$ of the amount of money on her card.

Mrs. Quaid: Brian, would you rephrase the relationship Kerry saw in the prob-lem statement between two of the quantites?

> Recording the list of quantities is a key support for developing quantitative reasoning because it keeps this distinction between a quantity and a number front and center in the discussion. It provides language support as students can refer to the list to talk about the relationships they see, and it provides a critical reference for students with memory issues.

Brian: OK. Kerry said the amount of money Camille spent was $\frac{1}{3}$ the amount of money she had to start.

Mrs. Quaid (*Recording the relationship*): Now that we have named many of the essential quantities and relationships, let's create some diagrams.

<u>Relationships</u>

The # of dollars Dan spent is $\frac{1}{2}$ the amount of money on Dan's card to start

The amount of money Camille has left is equal to the amount of money Dan has left

The amount of money Camille spent was $\frac{1}{3}$ the amount of money she had to start

Figure 3.12

PART 3: CREATE DIAGRAMS

Mrs. Quaid tells students that they will be creating a diagram that represents the important quantities and relationships from the video game shop gift card problem stem, and reminds them that they can refer to the lists she has just recorded.

Individual Think Time

Mrs. Quaid: You have two minutes of individual think time. I'm not expecting you to complete your diagram. This time is for you to start capturing the quantities and relationships in a diagram. You and your partner will make a final diagram together after this think time. To get started, ask yourself, *How much bigger or smaller is one quantity than another?* and *How can I show how much bigger or smaller one quantity is in my diagram?* (*She writes these questions on the board for reference.*)

Pairs

Mrs. Quaid pulls the class back together. She projects a slide with instructions and two sentence starters: "How did you represent _____?" and "I showed _____ by _____."

Mrs. Quaid: Great start. Turn to your partner and share how you've started to represent important problem information in your diagram. Use these sentence starters (*Pointing to the slide*) to help you describe how your diagram shows the quantities and relationships we have in our list. For example, ask your

---

Similarly, recording the relationships in the familiar (<u>Quantity A</u>) is (<u>relationship to</u>) (<u>Quantity B</u>) structure provides a memory and language support for students before they create diagrams that capture these relationships.

The individual think time provides all students an opportunity to practice reasoning quantitatively by thinking about how to represent quantities and relationships with a diagram. The ask-yourself questions provide a focus for students who need structure to get started.

partner, "How did you represent (*Pointing to an entry on the quantities list*) the number of dollars Dan spent?" When sharing your own diagram, explain how you tried to show quantities and relationships. So you might say, "I showed the relationships between (*Pointing to the quantities list again*) the amount of money Camille has left and the amount she had to start by. . . . " After you have explained your thinking, work together to create a diagram that you think best represents the important problem information. ⦿

Mrs. Quaid circulates, looking at the diagrams students are making and listening to their conversations. She notes which quantities and relationships students include in their diagrams and how accurately the relationships are represented—especially the one describing the equivalent balances on both gift cards in the end. She's looking for examples of student diagrams to select that collectively show the different quantities, that capture at least some of the important relationships between the quantities, and that represent the quantities and relationships differently from each other to model different ways to generate a diagram. She makes her choice, and asks three pairs of students to reproduce their diagrams on chart paper without any labels. The three diagrams are shown in Figures 3.13, 3.14, and 3.15.

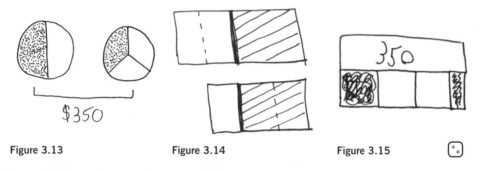

Figure 3.13   Figure 3.14   Figure 3.15   ⦿

PART 4: DISCUSS DIAGRAMS

Notice that Mrs. Quaid poses questions here and throughout the vignette about where in the diagram students can see the quantities, to focus students' attention on successfully interpreting the diagrams.

⦿ Note that Mrs. Quaid focuses partner conversations by providing two sentence starters and gesturing back to the recorded list of quantities. She then models using the sentence starters. This both keeps the mathematical focus on quantitative reasoning and provides language support to ELLs.

⦿ As she thinks about how to sequence the diagrams in the discussion, Mrs. Quaid decides to ask Charlie and Gloria to share their diagram first (Figure 3.13), because it can be used to identify many of the problem quantities and relationships, but they have omitted one critical one: that the amount left on both cards in the end is equal. Perhaps they forgot to include the relationship, or they are not yet able to represent it using a circle diagram, or they are not thinking flexibly about "the whole" when dealing with fractions. Mrs. Quaid decides that all three potential reasons would be important to sort out with the class.

Even after four or five times with the routine, students may not necessarily be able to capture quantities accurately, and this is one of the most common mistakes. However, a class can still learn from imperfect diagrams, especially if the information they do show accurately is easy to spot.

Individual Think Time and Pairs

Mrs. Quaid: Take thirty seconds to look at the diagram Charlie and Gloria created (Figure 3.16). What quantities or relationships from the problem stem do you see in their diagram?

Mrs. Quaid (*After thirty seconds*): Turn to your partner and share where you see these quantities (*Pointing to the list of quantities and relationships*) in Gloria and Charlie's diagram. ⟨•⟩

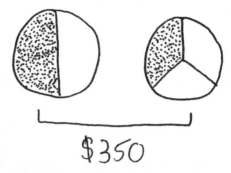

Figure 3.16

Share and Discuss

Mrs. Quaid (*Bringing the class back together*): Where do you see a quantity or relationship in Charlie and Gloria's diagram? Brian?

Brian (*Pointing from his seat*): We saw the amount of money that Dan spent and the amount of money Camille spent in the circles.

Mrs. Quaid: Can you and Sam come up here and use the pointer to show us where you see "the amount of money Dan spent and the amount of money Camille spent"? ⟨•⟩ ⟨•⟩

Brian and Sam approach the diagram. Brian points to the shaded third on the right-hand circle and Sam points to the unshaded half of the other circle (Figure 3.16).

Mrs. Quaid: So Brian, what quantity are you pointing to? And can you also say why you think it's that quantity?

Brian: This shaded part (*Pointing at Figure 3.16*) is the amount of money Camille spent because we know she spent a third of the money on her card. (*Pointing to each section*) One, two, three, and this one is shaded. So that's what she spent.

⟨•⟩ The individual think time and subsequent partner share provides students processing time so that they can notice features of the diagram and begin to think about how those features highlight a quantity or relationship. This processing time better positions all students to participate in the full-group share, although it is critical for some students who need additional processing time. The partner share is another processing vehicle as students can talk through their thinking and hear how another is seeing quantities. It also provides ELLs a lower stress opportunity to practice language development.

⟨•⟩ In the class discussion that follows, notice that Mrs. Quaid asks students who did not generate the diagram to help interpret it. This places all students squarely in the position of making sense of each other's quantitative reasoning. Not only is the class making sense of and explaining how Charlie and Gloria captured quantities and relationships in their diagram, Charlie and Gloria are now listening carefully to their classmates to see if their ideas are being accurately represented.

⟨•⟩ In the next part, Mrs. Quaid will use annotation to focus student attention on where quantities and relationships are found in the diagrams. This emphasizes the quantitative reasoning for all students, as well as provides essential visual supports for students who struggle to follow the full-group conversation, focus for easily distracted students, and reference for students with memory issues. Annotating helps ELLs follow the full-group discussion by including words and phrases in the annotations that support language production.

Mrs. Quaid: Who agrees with Brian that the shaded portion he's pointing to represents the amount of money Camille spent? (*All hands go up.*) OK, Brian, would you please label the shaded part? (*Brian draws an arrow to the shaded region and writes "amt. of $ Camille spent."*) Sam, while Brian is labeling that quantity, would you please talk to us about the quantity you pointed to?

Sam: This is the amount of money Dan spent because he spent half of the money on his card, and this is half (*Pointing to the whole circle and then the unshaded part*). [See Figure 3.17.]

Mrs. Quaid: So you're saying that the unshaded half is the amount of money Dan spent? (*Sam nods.*) (*To the class*) Let me see thumbs up if you agree, down if you disagree, and sideways if you're not sure. Is the amount or number of dollars Dan spent represented by the unshaded portion Sam is pointing to? (*Mrs. Quaid scans the room. Most students agree. Only Meaghan and Kerry have their thumbs to the side.*) Kerry, Meaghan, you are not yet convinced. Say why you're not convinced or ask Sam a question.

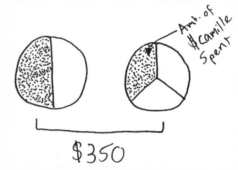

Figure 3.17

Kerry: Well, there's two halves. I don't know why Sam picked the unshaded half for the amount of money Dan spent? Couldn't it be the other half?

Sam: Oh. Yeah. It should be the other half.

Mrs. Quaid: "It should be the other half"? Make an argument for why the amount of money Dan spent should be the shaded half.

Sam: Because in this one (*Pointing to the other circle*), the amount Camille spent was shaded, so the amount of money Dan spent should be shaded too. I mean, they're both half but the shading should mean the same thing, so the amount Dan spent is the shaded half.

Mrs. Quaid: Maria, can you restate Sam's reasoning?

Maria: I think. Sam said that because the shading represented money spent in the other circle, it should represent money spent in this circle, too. So the amount Dan spent should be the shaded half.

Mrs. Quaid: Kerry, Meaghan, do you agree?

Kerry: Yes.

Meaghan: Uh-huh.

Mrs. Quaid: Charlie and Gloria, this is your diagram. Why did you shade the two circles the way you did?

Gloria: To show the money Dan and Camille spent. (⚀)

Mrs. Quaid: Sam, would you please label the shaded half? (*Sam draws an arrow to the shaded half of the circle and writes "amt. of $ Dan spent" then sits down.*) [See Figure 3.18.] (⚃)

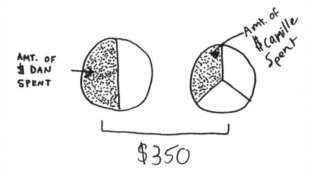

AMT. OF $ DAN SPENT

Amt. of $ Camille Spent

$350

Figure 3.18

Mrs. Quaid: While Sam is labeling the amount of money Dan spent, who can tell us where the total amount of money on both cards is represented in the diagram? (⚅)

James: The $350.

Mrs. Quaid: And what part of the diagram represents the $350, the total amount on both video cards to start?

James: Um, the two circles.

(⚀) The goal is for students to learn how aspects of a diagram can illustrate quantities and relationships. The consistency of shading is an important point and so Mrs. Quaid draws students' attention to it ("So you're saying that the unshaded half is the amount of money Dan spent?"), checks to see who agrees or disagrees ("Is the amount or number of dollars Dan spent represented by the unshaded portion Sam is pointing to?"), presses Sam to provide justification for why he changed his mind ("they're both half but the shading should mean the same thing, so the amount Dan spent is the shaded half"), has Maria restate Sam's reasoning ("because the shading represented money spent in the other circle, it should represent money spent in this circle, too"), and finally has Gloria confirm ("To show the money Dan and Camille spent"). All this provides multiple passes at this important idea and thus multiple processing opportunities for students.

(⚃) Annotation is helpful because it provides focus for students with attention difficulties and because it helps ELLs and students who are weak auditory processors follow a verbal math discussion. Note that annotation is also a mathematical tool (MP5)—Gloria and Charles used shading to represent quantities related to spent money. The first couple of times she led the routine, Mrs. Quaid did all the annotating during the full-group discussions, but now she is turning over more of the annotating to the students to help them build their annotation skills.

(⚅) Having Sam annotate the diagram helps solidify the idea for him and allows Mrs. Quaid to continue facilitating the conversation. The annotation is a visual reminder of the quantity the shading represents.

Mrs. Quaid: "The two circles," OK. Other thoughts?

Kerry: The line (*Gestures, tracing the "line" in the air*).

Mrs. Quaid: Which line? Come up and show us the line you are talking about.

Kerry (*Walking up to the diagram and tracing the bracket with her finger*): This line.

Mrs. Quaid: OK, so the line or bracket underneath the two circles. Why do the bracket and the two circles show the total amount of money on both cards at the start? James, why don't you start the explanation and Kerry, because you are standing next to the diagram, you can point to what James is saying. ⊙

James: Well, one circle is the money on Dan's card (*Kerry traces the left circle*) and the other shows the amount on Camille's card (*Kerry traces the second circle*). The line, er, bracket (*Pauses*) it kinda connects the circles (*Kerry shows the connection with her finger*).

Mrs. Quaid: Kerry?

Kerry: Yeah, we know both circles show the amount on each card to start and the bracket is sort of like an arrow pointing to the circles.

Mrs. Quaid: Great, would you please label the quantity? (*Kerry writes, "Total amt. of money on both cards at the start" and sits down.*) [See Figure 3.19.]

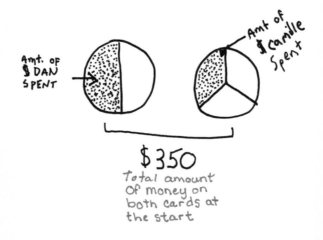

Figure 3.19

⊙ Asking James to explain and Kerry to point puts both students in the position of considering each other's thinking. Kerry must listen carefully to what James is saying so that she can point appropriately and James must watch Kerry to make sure she is following his line of reasoning. This will slow down James' explanation and makes Kerry's pointing more deliberate, which will support both ELLs and slower processors.

Mrs. Quaid: One last question before we move onto another diagram. (*Pointing to the recorded relationship "the amount of money Camille has left is equal to the amount of money Dan has left"*): Where in this diagram do you see this relationship between the amount of money left on Camille's card and the amount of money left on Dan's card? Take ten seconds of individual think time. (*She pauses.*) OK, turn and talk to your shoulder buddy. Where do you see the relationship between the number of dollars left on Camille's card and the number of dollars left on Dan's card? ⊡

Mrs. Quaid tours the room, listening in on student conversations to determine who can see that the unshaded regions—the circle parts that represent the remaining amounts on Dan and Camille's cards—are not the same size.

Mrs. Quaid (*Bringing the class back together*): Maria, what did you and Meaghan decide? Where is the relationship between the number of dollars left on Camille's card and the number of dollars left on Dan's card in this diagram?

Maria: It's there, but it's not right.

Mrs. Quaid: What's there?

Maria: The amount of money left on the video store cards. It's the white part. The amount of money left on Dan's card is the white half and Camille's is the two empty parts on the other circle. (*Mrs. Quaid moves to the diagram and points as Maria explains her thinking.*)

Mrs. Quaid (*Noticing Sam is distracted*): Sam, can you restate what Maria said about these (*Pointing*) white or unshaded parts of the diagram?

Sam: Oh, uh. The unshaded parts represent the amount left on each card.

Mrs. Quaid: OK and, Maria, you said something about "not being right."

Maria: Yeah, Meaghan was saying that the amount Dan and Camille have left is the same but it's not the same in the circle.

Mrs. Quaid: Kerry, what does Maria mean when she says "the amount Dan and Camille have left is not the same in the circle"?

Kerry: They're not the same size.

Mrs. Quaid: What's not the same size?

Kerry: The unshaded parts of the circles are not the same size and they would need to be to show that the amount Dan and Camille had left was the same. The diagram shows that the amount Camille has left is more than the amount Dan has left. (*Mrs. Quaid points to the diagrams as Kerry speaks.*)

Mrs. Quaid: OK, so this diagram captured many important quantities from the problem stem. We could see the total amount of money on both cards, the amount of money each person spent, and the number of dollars both Dan and Camille had left. One relationship that was not captured in the

⊡ Notice that Mrs. Quaid waits until students are familiar with the diagram and the various quantities and relationships represented therein to press the issue of the misrepresented equivalence relationship. This relationship between the remaining amounts left on each card is the crux of the word problem because it's this relationship that allows you to ultimately determine the values of all the other quantities.

diagram accurately was the relationship between the number of dollars left on each card at the end. Let's look at another diagram to see if that missing relationship—as well as the others we've identified—are represented. [See Figure 3.20.]

A Second Round of Individual Think Time and Pairs

Mrs. Quaid: Take a look at this diagram (*Pointing to the diagram Brian and Sam created*). Twenty seconds of individual think time. What relationships do you see represented in this diagram? You may want to use our list (*Pointing to the relationships record*) as a reference.

Mrs. Quaid: OK, in a minute I am going to ask you to turn and talk with your partner. But I want to give some instructions first. This time when you talk, I want you to talk about how you found the relationships in the diagram. Here are two sentence frames that I want you to use to focus your discussion.

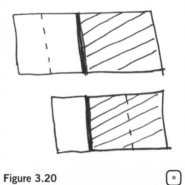

Figure 3.20

"The relationship is _____ so I looked for _____."

"I noticed _____ so I looked for two quantities that _____."

Mrs. Quaid: The first one is for students who started by looking at a relationship on our list. Raise your hand if during your think time, you started by looking at a relationship and then tried to find it in the diagram. (*Some students raise their hands.*) So you should use the first sentence frame that starts with what you knew about how the two quantities were related. Raise your hand if you started by looking at the diagram first. (*Other students raise their hands.*) OK, you should use the second sentence frame that begins with what you noticed in the diagram and how that described a relationship between two quantities. For example, if we were using this frame for the last diagram I might say, "I noticed the bracket above the $350 so I was looking for two quantities that added to $350." If you can't remember where you starting looking first, consider both frames and pick one.

Mrs. Quaid decides to shift to discussing Brian and Sam's diagram (Figure 3.20) because it accurately captures the equivalence relationship (and all other quantities and relationships) and will help students see that Camille had to have started with less money on her card. Also the second diagram makes use of rectangles, and that allows for a conversation about how different shapes can be easier or harder to partition, to notice equivalencies, and so on.

Notice that the first sentence frame supports the reasoning of a student who started by considering the written relationship statements. This could be a student who struggles conceptually and thus is helped by starting from the context description to connect to the representation. It also supports students for whom language is a strength. The second sentence frame provides entry for students who started by considering the diagram. This may be an ELL who finds easier entry through the visual or a strong visual processor. For beginning English speakers, substituting simpler sentence starters such as "I knew _____" and "I saw _____" may be more appropriate.

Partners share their thinking. Mrs. Quaid tours the room, listening in. She hears Charlie and Gloria talking about how the same amount was shaded in each of the rectangles. Because this observation is key to identifying the equivalence relationship, she decides to call on Charlie and Gloria first.

Mrs. Quaid (*Pulling the class back together*): Charlie and Gloria, why don't you start us off? What's a relationship you saw represented in this diagram? Please use one of the sentence frames when you share.

Gloria: We noticed the equal shading on the top and bottom, so we looked for two quantities that were the same. So we picked the second one, the amount of money Dan and Camille had in the end is the same.

Mrs. Quaid: Who else noticed that these shaded portions (*Pointing*) of both bars were the same size? (*Mrs. Quaid sees several hands go up.*) Nguyen, what relationship did Gloria and Charlie connect to what they noticed?

Nguyen (*Looking up at the list of relationships she reads*): The amount of money Camille has left is equal to the amount of money Dan has left. (*Mrs. Quaid places a star next to the relationship on their list.*) [See Figure 3.21.]

<u>Relationships</u>

The # of dollars Dan spent is $\frac{1}{2}$ the amount of money on Dan's card to start

The amount of money Camille has left is equal to the amount of money Dan has left

The amount of money Camille spent was $\frac{1}{3}$ the amount of money she had to start

Figure 3.21

Mrs. Quaid: Hoang, what quantity does this shaded portion show or represent (*Pointing to the shading on the top bar then motioning to the recorded list of quantities and relationships*)? The number of. . . .

Hoang (*Looking at the list of quantities on the board*): The number of dollars Dan has left.

Mrs. Quaid: And Hoang, what quantity does this shaded portion show or represent (*Pointing to the shading on the bottom bar*)?

Hoang (*Looking at the list of quantities on the board*): Amount of money Camille had left.

Mrs. Quaid: Why is this shaded part (*Pointing*) the number of dollars Dan has left?

Hoang: Half . . . the number of dollars Dan spent is half. (*Pauses*) Half left. (*Pauses*) The number of dollars Dan have left is half.

Mrs. Quaid: The number of dollars Dan has left is half—of what?

Hoang (*Looking back at the lists of quantities and relationships*): The bar (*Pauses*) the amount of money Dan have (*Pauses*) to start.

Mrs. Quaid: Who can summarize Hoang's argument that the shading in the top bar represents the amount of money Dan has left? ⦿

Discussion of this diagram and the third diagram continues with students explaining how the quantities and relationships from the video store gift card problem are represented in the diagrams.

PART 5: REFLECT ON QUANTITATIVE THINKING

Revisit Thinking Goal

Mrs. Quaid stops the full-group share with ten minutes left so that her students have enough time to reflect on what they have learned about reasoning quantitatively and abstractly. She begins the reflection by reminding students why they were capturing quantities. She then gives them two sentence starters to use to share what they learned.

When looking for quantities in a word problem, I learned to _____.

When analyzing a diagram, I learned to pay attention to _____ because _____.

Individual Write Time and Pairs

Mrs. Quaid lays out the steps for the reflection and provides two sentence starters. As students write and share, she tours the room reading what students wrote.

Mrs. Quaid: OK, go ahead and share what you learned about reasoning abstractly and quantitatively with your partner. (*Mrs. Quaid listens in as partners share their thoughts.*)

As usual, different students have identified different aspects of the avenue of thinking to remember. Mrs. Quaid decides to ask Sam, Charlie, and Meaghan to share because the primary goal of the activity was to learn how to represent relationships visually on a diagram and their reflections speak to aspects of a diagram that can communicate a relationship.

Share ⦂

Mrs. Quaid: Sam, please start us off.

Sam: When analyzing a diagram, I learned to pay attention to the shading because it has to mean the same thing. (*Mrs. Quaid adds Sam's reflection to*

⦿ Mrs. Quaid noted that Hoang and his partner had also seen the equivalence relationships in the shading in Brian and Sam's diagram. Hoang had an opportunity to communicate with his partner about this connection. At this point in the routine, Mrs. Quaid presses Hoang to share his thinking in the full group. In doing so, Mrs. Quaid points to the shading as she poses her question; she gestures to the recorded lists of quantities and relationships and provides the sentence starter, "The number of _____." These actions support Hoang as he shares his quantitative reasoning (i.e., how he sees quantities and relationships in a diagram) and continues to develop more precise language to describe mathematical quantities and relationships.

⦂ Teachers of English learners sometimes choose to pair-write-share instead of write-pair-share, finding that talking with a partner before writing helps ELLs get their ideas down on paper more easily.

the list of things people have learned from previous Capturing Quantities activities.) [See Figure 3.22.]

Mrs. Quaid: Charlie?

Charlie: Pay attention to parts of the diagram that are the same size because then I know the quantities are equal. *(Mrs. Quaid records.)* [See Figure 3.22.]

Mrs. Quaid: One more, Meaghan?

Meaghan: Pay attention to brackets because they will connect quantities. *(Mrs. Quaid records.)* [See Figure 3.22.]

Mrs. Quaid: Great. So the next time you are trying to represent important information in a diagram or you are interpreting a diagram, think like a mathematician and pay attention to shading, parts that are the same size, and brackets!

Think Like a Mathematician

Pay attention to . . .

- The things you can count
- The numbers because they are clues for quantities
- Shading on a diagram
- Equal parts on a diagram
- Brackets on a diagram

Ask yourself . . .

- What can I count?
- How many?
- How much bigger is the quantity?

Figure 3.22

Important Takeaways

Within the vignette you've just read, there are several important points we'd like to underscore about developing quantitative reasoning through the routine. Think about how these relate to your own instruction as you use this routine:

- Students are accustomed to looking for key numbers in a problem, so build from that habit to help students learn to also identify quantities and relationships. Support students as they transition from focusing on numbers toward focusing on quantities by restating a student's idea in the context of one of the sentence frames, initially using as much of the student's own language as you can. Then be mindful of striking a balance between using students' own language for ideas that they contribute to the discussion and modeling the use of quantitative language by echoing the sentence starters and sentence frames.

- Naming quantities and relationships and building the surrounding language helps develop quantitative reasoning. So, allow time to have different students paraphrase what others are adding to the discussion. This not only ensures that the student who is speaking can summarize the thinking of others, but it also gives the students who are listening an additional opportunity to process the language and the content of the discussion.

- The diagrams that students create will become more purposeful and robust with repeated experiences in Capturing Quantities. As students gain proficiency in identifying implied quantities and "hidden relationships" in representations, they will also begin to make purposeful decisions around the types of representations they choose—for example, distinguishing diagrams that capture relationships between parts and parts from those that show relationships between parts and wholes. As students analyze a variety of representations in the full group, they will broaden their repertoire of visual representations—single bar models, diagrams that involve multiple bars, circle graphs, and so on.

In the next chapter, we'll look at an instructional routine that develops another of the avenues of thinking: Thinking structurally. You'll see some of these same teacher moves reflected in that routine as well.

Connecting Representations

An Instructional Routine to Support Students Thinking
About and with Mathematical Structure

In Mr. Smith's sixth-grade classroom, students had been working individually on a problem set involving area and surface area. The class had been discussing how to organize their work, so Mr. Smith was watching to see what students did to find the area of the figure (Figure 4.1).

When they finished, Mr. Smith provided answers to the problems and asked students to correct their work with a partner. Annika and Matthew were confused because they both had incorrect answers to one of the problems. Mr. Smith said the answer was 52 square units. Annika calculated 44 square units and Matthew had 48 square units. Annika checked her work carefully; she was confident that she had not made any computation errors. She pointed to her organized work (Figure 4.2), and reviewed her calculations with Matthew, explaining to him that she listed each partial area, and added them together by finding friendly sums.

Together, they looked at Matthew's work (Figure 4.3). Annika had difficulty following it at first. It seemed like Matthew had done more work than she had. Matthew explained that he set up all of the smaller area problems, did all the multiplication, then all of the addition. Annika quickly noticed that Matthew made an error when he multiplied the second 3×4. Matthew looked back in disbelief; of course he knew that 3×4 is 12! He said he must have thought it was 2×4.

Figure 4.1

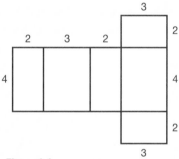

$2 \times 4 = 8$
$3 \times 4 = 12$ } 20
$3 \times 2 = 6$
$3 \times 4 = 12$ } 12
$2 \times 3 = 6$ } 12

$20 + 24 = \boxed{44}$

Figure 4.2

$$4 \times 2 + 3 \times 4 + 2 \times 4 + 3 \times 2 + 3 \times 4 + 2 \times 3$$
$$8 + 3 \times 4 + 8 + 6 + 8 + 6$$
$$8 + 12 + 8 + 6 + 8 + 6$$
$$20 + 8 + 6 + 8 + 6$$
$$28 + 12 + 8$$
$$48$$

Figure 4.3

Mr. Smith listened in as Matthew and Annika discussed their approaches. He sighed; despite the time they'd spent on organizing work more carefully, these two—and numerous other students in the class—were still having trouble although they tried to organize their work well! He didn't want to keep spending the time going over this material; the class really needed to move on to the next unit, or they would be way behind by winter break.

In the previous scenario, each student dove into calculations and wound up doing arithmetic that was not efficient (or correct!). Keeping track of many calculations is challenging for many students, and multistep arithmetic that involves transposing numbers often leads to errors for many students as well. Annika's work was very well organized, but Annika didn't connect the calculations to the net. Matthew organized his work as well, but organization alone wasn't enough to keep him from making other errors. Organizing your work is an important skill in mathematics, but it can bypass a critical part of making sense of the problem that sits squarely in the "structural" avenue of thinking: getting students to move beyond long extended calculations and begin to consider how to organize the mathematical parts of the problem.

Mathematical thinkers who are approaching a problem from a structural avenue of thinking are trying to determine how a mathematical "object"—such as a numeric expression, an equation, function, graph, or geometric figure—is behaving; how to think about the mathematical object in terms of its parts; and how seeing those parts may help suggest a particular approach to solving the problem. In this chapter, we'll look at what it means to think structurally in math class, and introduce the *Connecting Representations* instructional routine to support all students' development and use of structural thinking.

What Does It Mean to "Think Structurally"?

In Chapter 1, we got an initial glimpse of a student who thinks structurally, as we followed Stephanie's progress through a mathematics problem. Now let's go into a little more depth about what it means to think structurally. To do so, please take a moment to work through the following example (Figure 4.4) yourself.

Consider the two figures and the expressions for the area of these figures. Both figures have the same area, and each expression results in the same total area.

Which expression goes with which figure? Be ready to explain why.

Without completing any calculations, see if you can connect each visual to one of the expressions so that the expression represents the particular color-coding shown in the figures. (One of the three expressions does not correspond to the figures.) Then see if you can justify the connection you chose. As you think through the task, ask yourself, "What are the pieces of the figure or of the expression, and how do they connect to the other representation?"

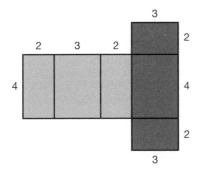

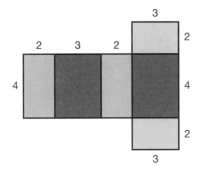

A) $2(2 \times 4) + 2(3 \times 4) + 2(3 \times 2)$

B) $4(2 + 3 + 2 + 3) + 2(3 \times 2)$

C) $4(2 + 3 + 2) + 3(2 + 4 + 2)$

Figure 4.4

What did you pay attention to as you considered the visual? Did you key in on the color, or did you gravitate toward the numbers or the shapes? Or maybe you started with the three expressions. If so, what did you think was significant about the expressions? Did you notice how many "chunks" made up each expression? Did you look at the numbers first or did you focus on the operations as your entry point?

As you keyed in on different "pieces" of either the expression or the figures, you may have asked yourself one or more of the following questions:

- How many "chunks" does this expression consist of, and what are they?
- What are the operations? And what could they represent in this visual?
- What does the color have to do with the corresponding mathematical expression?
- How are the measurements of the shape connected to the numeric expression?

The kind of reasoning represented by these questions is an example of thinking structurally, and the problem—to connect a numeric expression to a visual without completing any calculations—was designed to encourage you to think in that way. You were asked to use the given information and make sense of it to find similarities between mathematical representations that at first might not have appeared to be similar, an indication of thinking structurally.

An Example of Structural Thinking

Let's consider how one student, Gina, thought about this example.

She notices that the irregular shapes are made up of multiple rectangles. The first one has two "chunks": a gray one and a blue one. The gray one is a "4 by $(2 + 3 + 2)$" rectangle and the blue one is a "3 by $(2 + 4 + 2)$" rectangle (Figure 4.5).

So instead of finding the area of each little individual rectangle, she starts looking for the area of the total gray space—a "4 by $(2 + 3 + 2)$" rectangle—and the area of the total blue space—a "3 by $(2 + 4 + 2)$" rectangle. She notices that would be expression C: $4(2 + 3 + 2) + 3(2 + 4 + 2)$.

She then pays attention to the other choices for numeric expressions and notices that expression B, like expression C, has two numeric "chunks" getting added together, but expression A is different—it has three chunks: $2(2 \times 4) + 2(3 \times 4) + 2(3 \times 2)$.

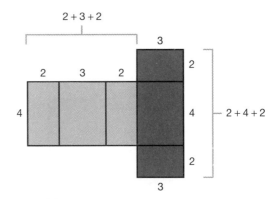

Figure 4.5

She sees that each piece in expression A involves multiplication, and she knows that she can think of multiplication as some number of groups of some amount. So she thinks of $2(2 \times 4)$ as two (2×4)s, and mentally expands expression A into $(2 \times 4) + (2 \times 4) + (3 \times 4)$ $+ (3 \times 4) + (3 \times 2) + (3 \times 2)$.

From prior work with area, she knows that she can connect each of those products to the area of a rectangle. Studying the second figure more closely, she looks for three pairs of same-size rectangles, and confirms for herself that they are there in the figure (Figure 4.6).

Notice that Gina did not immediately just begin calculating "the answer" to the expression, reducing it to one number. Students often focus first on the numbers and, more often than not, will start calculating right away, in this case reducing an expression like $4(2 + 3 + 2) + 3(2 + 4 + 2)$ to $4(7) + 3(8)$ or 52. Although simplifying may be what they are most accustomed to doing, it is not very helpful for connecting or creating representations. By keeping the expression in its expanded form, Gina is able to connect each part of the visual figure to the parts of the expression.

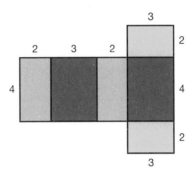

Figure 4.6

It turns out that the operations and grouping symbols provide the clues that tell you how the numbers and space might be organized, thereby providing a window to the underlying structure.

Chunk, Change, Connect

Gina's thinking includes three useful actions that arise (often together) as part of thinking structurally:

Chunk: When Gina shifts her attention from six separate rectangles to seeing two rectangles, she is "chunking" the figure. Similarly, when she notices the two parts in expressions B and C and the three parts in expression A, she is chunking the expression. This capacity to chunk or organize complicated objects into recognizable pieces can often help you notice some underlying similarity or structure.

Change: When Gina realizes that she could think of $2(2 \times 4)$ as two (2×4)s and mentally expands expression A into $(2 \times 4) + (2 \times 4) + (3 \times 4) + (3 \times 4) + (3 \times 2)$ $+ (3 \times 2)$, she is changing the form of the expression. Changing the form of a representation—either an expression or a figure—is another action that can help you notice some underlying similarity or structure.

Connect: Gina notices a connection between something in the problem and some mathematics with which she is already familiar when she realizes that she can connect each of the products to the area of a rectangle. She then looks for three pairs of same-size rectangles. Looking for possible mathematical connections is a third action that can help you use what you've noticed about the structure to solve a problem.

You may want to see if you can chunk, change, and connect to come up with the visual representation that would correspond to the remaining expression.

$$\text{B) } 4(2 + 3 + 2 + 3) + 2(3 \times 2)$$

Asking yourself questions like the following can help you connect the expression to the figure:

- How many chunks does this expression consist of, and what are they?
- What are the operations? And how could they connect to this visual?

These three actions and their accompanying ask-yourself questions form the primary goals for students as they develop structural thinking throughout the Connecting Representations routine.

An Overview of the Connecting Representations Routine

Connecting Representations is an instructional routine designed to focus students' attention on mathematical structure in equivalent representations by providing them with two sets of representations to interpret and match, much like the example at the beginning of this chapter. The representations may initially look nothing like each other, yet turn out to represent the same relationship or value or behave in the same way. Students then find and connect the structural elements common to both representations. This often requires interpreting complicated objects (e.g., expressions, diagrams, calculations, graphs, and so on) by chunking one or more of their parts together and/or changing the form of numbers, expressions, or visuals to uncover mathematical form.

The Steps of the Routine

The Connecting Representations routine has five parts to it. Recall from Chapter 2 that each routine begins with an initial introduction to the routine (Part 1), including sharing a mathematical thinking goal with your students, and ends with a student reflection on how they developed their mathematical thinking and how they might use it in future problems (Part 5).

Parts 2, 3, and 4 are unique to this routine. In the Connecting Representations routine, students analyze two sets of corresponding representations to look for and identify structural similarities in order to identify "matching partners" and describe how the representations are related (Part 2). One representation is left without a matching partner, so students use what they now understand about the structural similarities to create a corresponding representation for that remaining one (Part 3). Students then share and discuss the new representation (Part 4).

These next sections provide a brief overview of the five parts of the routine. Later, we provide a classroom illustration of what this routine looks like in action, and we'll highlight particular supports for special populations.

Part 1: Launch the Routine

When launching the routine, the teacher identifies the thinking goal and reviews the steps of the routine. It is important that students understand that they are developing structural thinking during this learning experience. The goal is not just to match the representations, but also to name the thinking behind the connections that is applicable to a multitude of problems.

Steps for Part 1

1. Display and explain the thinking goal. For example, you might say, "Today we are going to learn how to think like mathematicians. We are going to learn how to use mathematical structure to connect mathematical representations that at first don't look alike." (See Chapter 7 for examples of thinking goals you can use with this routine.)

2. Display and explain the flow and format of the routine. Help students understand that they will be interpreting sets of representations individually, making connections with a partner, discussing connections in the full group, creating a representation through a think-pair-share, and, finally, reflecting on their learning.

Part 2: Interpret and Connect Representations

The purpose of this second part of the routine is for students to notice and begin to interpret important features of the different representations and to match representations based on their interpretations. Initially, students work independently to interpret representations and look for structural elements they can use to connect them. Students then work with a partner to share what they noticed and make connections between representations. Finally, in a whole-class discussion, the teacher prompts students to articulate the observations about structure that underlie and justify their connections. As students rephrase and refine their thinking, the teacher annotates the representations to highlight the structural connections.

Steps for Part 2

Individual Think Time

1. Present sets of representations to students and give them 20–30 seconds of private think time to decipher one representation and begin looking for its match among a set of representations of another type. As you send students off to think individually, pose an ask-yourself question to focus their attention toward structural thinking.

Pair

2. Have students share how they are interpreting the representations with a partner and continue working together to connect representations. Circulate to listen in on their conversations, noting which representations students gravitate toward. Listen for evidence of chunking the representation into pieces, interpreting and connecting the pieces, and/or changing the form of a representation to match an interpretation or another representation.

Share and Discuss

3. Select a pair of students to come forward and share two representations they connected and what they noticed that helped them see the connection. Ask one student to be the speaker and the other student to point and gesture to the corresponding representation. Use sentence starters and frames like the following to support the share-out:

   We noticed _____ so we looked for _____.

   We knew _____ so we connected _____ to _____.

   Ask a different pair to restate or rephrase the ideas, including what the first pair paid attention to and how that helped them make the connection. Ask the full group whether they agree or disagree with the connection that has been made and what was most convincing (or not convincing) about the explanation.

Annotate

4. Ask a new pair to summarize the thinking. During this summary highlight or have students highlight the connections through color, symbols, and/or words.

5. Repeat with another representation as time permits.

Part 3: Create Representations

The purpose of this third part of the routine is for students to apply the structural think-ing they have named to create a new matching representation. Students consider a repre-sentation for which there is no match and then work to create a matching representation.

Steps for Part 3

Individual Think Time

1. Orient students' attention to the remaining unmatched representation. Ask an orienting question like "What do you notice about this representation?" or "How can you chunk this representation into pieces you know?"

Pair

2. Have students share their initial thinking and work together to create a matching representation.

3. While the pairs work:

   • Circulate, watching and listening for evidence of structural thinking (i.e., chunking, changing, and connecting).

   • Determine which representation you will have the class discuss.

Part 4: Discuss Representations

Students now have an opportunity to discuss a new representation that a pair has cre-ated. This discussion helps students practice articulating the common structure underly-ing the representations.

This discussion follows a think-pair-share format as well, as students are given brief individual think time to consider the new representation, then discuss it in pairs. The full discussion then focuses on clearly articulating the connection between the represen-tations. In this round of discussion, students have an opportunity to help annotate the representations to highlight the connections.

Steps for Part 4

Individual Think Time

1. Post one representation for the class to consider. Give students a few seconds of individual think time to consider the representation and how it connects to the "unmatched" representation.

Pair

2. Prompt students to talk with a partner to determine if the representations match and be able to explain why or why not.

Share–Discuss and Annotate

3. Ask a pair of students who did not create the representation to explain the connection between the representations. Use sentence starters and frames like the following to support the discussion:

   They noticed _____ so they _____.

   They chunked _____.

   They changed _____ to _____.

   These starters keep the focus on identifying, then making use of, the structure underlying each representation.

4. Ask a second pair to come forward to rephrase and annotate the representations to highlight the matching features.

Part 5: Reflect on Structural Thinking

In the last part of the routine, students reflect on what they have learned about structural thinking that will help them in their future problem solving and math learning. If time is running short, it is better to discuss one fewer representation and save time for the reflection.

Steps for Part 5

Individual Write Time

1. Frame the reflection by revisiting the thinking goal for this routine. Provide students with sentence starters and frames to focus their reflection (e.g. "When interpreting a representation, I learned to pay attention to _____" or

"When connecting representations, I learned to ask myself _____" or "A new mathematical connection I made is _____." Give students 1–3 minutes of quiet writing time to reflect and complete a sentence frame.

Pair

2. Have students share what they wrote with a partner. Listen in as partners share and select two or three ideas related to the thinking goal to be shared in the full group.

Share

3. Have two or three students share what they learned about interpreting and connecting representations. Record the statements and post for future reference.

The entire routine-at-a-glance is shown in Figure 4.7. As you look at the routines across these chapters, note the parallels between the flows of each routine; this can help you become familiar with them more easily.

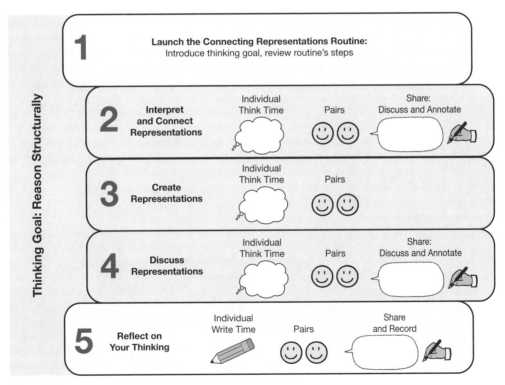

Figure 4.7

Essential Strategies in the Routine

As in the previous routine, although all the essential strategies are involved, the essential strategies of annotation and sentence frames and starters are particularly crucial for providing focus and access in this routine.

Essential Strategies

- Ask-yourself questions
- Annotation
- Sentence frames and sentence starters
- Four Rs: repeat, rephrase, reword, record

Annotation

This routine uses annotation throughout to develop students' structural thinking. The teacher and/or students annotate each of three pairs of representations to highlight the common underlying structure and make structural connections between them explicit. Within Connecting Representations, students share and make sense of each match through multiple opportunities for discourse. Annotation then serves the important purpose of creating a record, or "visual residue" of the discus-

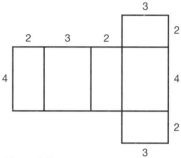

Figure 4.8

sion, through the use of color-coding, drawing arrows and dotted lines, and labeling the visuals. The annotations remain for students' reference. This can be especially important for students with attention difficulties.

As an example, let's look back at the example from the beginning of the chapter and explore an annotation for a new connection between the visual representation and a numeric expression. Consider how the following annotation provides an explicit connection between the area of the figure (Figure 4.8) and the expression, $4 \cdot 13$.

The annotation captures how someone might chunk the figure and change the form of the original figure (Figure 4.9). The color shows the horizontal chunk of the

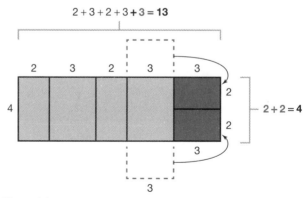

Figure 4.9

original figure in gray, and the two same-size chunks that create the "wings" of the original figure outlined in blue.

The dotted lines and arrows indicate the translation of the two original 2×3 rectangles from the wings to the right of the gray rectangle. Now, the newly created figure is one long rectangle with dimensions 4×13. The equations along the length and width of the rectangle make the dimensions of the side lengths explicit by mapping the font color onto the color of the figure. That way, we can clearly see the length and width of 13 and 4. This robust annotation allows *all* students to see explicit structural connections between the representations.

Look for the use of annotation in particular in:

- Part 2 when the whole class shares the connections between the representations
- Part 4 when the whole class analyzes a student-created representation and works to make the structural connections explicit.

Sentence Frames and Sentence Starters

The sentence frames and sentence starters in this routine are specifically designed to focus students' attention on seeing and describing the structural similarities between different representations and to model the language to talk about these similarities. Sentence frames such as "I noticed _____ and connected it to _____ because _____" move students beyond simply listing the steps they followed or naming the connection they made and focus their discussion on how they saw the connection between the corresponding representations. Sentence starters such as "They chunked _____" or "They changed _____ to _____" model the language the class is developing to talk about these structural similarities.

Look for examples of sentence frames and sentence starters in particular in:

- Part 2 when partners share their thinking with each other, and again when partners share a connection they've made in the full-group discussion
- Part 4 when the whole class interprets and explains the structural connections between a given representation and one created by a classmate.

Challenges, Opportunities, and Supports for Students with Specific Needs

Three features of the "structural" avenue of thinking are the actions we discussed in Chapter 1: chunk, change, and connect. All three provide valuable opportunities for special populations.

Students with Learning Disabilities

For students who struggle to notice structural similarities, using structural thinking to solve problems may seem mystifying or even magical. On the other hand, this avenue of thinking can feel refreshing to many students; it often eliminates the necessity for lengthy procedures that tax students' working memory and organizational skills and therefore cause errors in students' work.

This routine models structural thinking and breaks it down into manageable parts, two teaching strategies that are frequently referenced to support students with learning disabilities. Students start by interpreting representations provided to them—a receptive function—and work to make a first match. The class shares and discusses the basis for this match, and the teacher helps students rephrase, reword, and annotate. Students have multiple opportunities to develop and refine their thinking and the language to describe their thinking within the same connection. They then create a representation to complete the third match—a productive function. This gradual approach from receptive functions to productive functions scaffolds the development of structural thinking. The routine uses sentence frames and starters to help students articulate what they've noticed about mathematical structure. Throughout the routine, students learn from each other's approaches to noticing and describing mathematical structure, with the teacher helping to clarify; these approaches serve as models to develop the thinking.

This routine capitalizes on multiple representations to deepen mathematical understanding and to provide multiple entry points into the problem for a wide range of learners. It's important to select one of the sets of representations to play to the strengths of as many of your students with learning disabilities as you can. Then think about selecting the other set of representations in areas that may not be as strong, so that you can use the two types of representations to develop students' "math muscles" in their area of weakness.

For instance, strong visual-spatial learners can capitalize on interpreting a graph or visual representation before connecting it to an abstract algebraic expression that may be more challenging for them. Students who are more comfortable verbally can start from verbal descriptions and move to a visual representation that may be more challenging for them. Students helped by a relevant problem context may interpret a problem situation before connecting it to a corresponding representation.

During the full-group discussions in Part 2 and Part 4, students use a specific format for sharing structural connections between representations. One student is designated to point and gesture toward the representations (silently!) while another student describes the connections. This design allows reluctant students an opportunity to participate in the full group by assuming the silent role. For other students, the peer support encourages their participation in the full-group discussion. The design for sharing supports student participation and ensures a multimodal full-group discussion.

Supporting Students with Learning Disabilities When Using This Routine

- Provide multiple passes at articulating the underlying structure between representations using the Four Rs.

- Reference sentence frames and starters to prompt students to articulate observations that sparked the structural thinking and that can be applied again in other math problems.
- Use annotation to make structural connections explicit for students and to provide visual residue of the mathematical discussions.
- Choose representations that support students' learning strengths.
- Support students' participation in full-group discussions by defining partner roles.

English Language Learners

Connecting Representations epitomizes our guiding principle that the development of the math practices happens in language-rich environments. The same language that supports the development of structural thinking poses challenges for English language learners (ELLs). However, throughout this routine, whenever language is spoken, it is also supported with gestures, annotation, and/or recording. So although oral language plays an essential role in the instructional routine, there are multimodal supports that accompany the spoken language.

When students consider the two types of representations in front of them—visual and verbal, verbal and numeric, and so on—they draw upon two modalities. Students then surround the representations with gestures, color, annotations, and language, providing another opportunity for multimodal learning.

As students share their structural thinking, they revisit and refine their language through multiple think-pair-shares. The routine ends with the teacher recording the structural thinking supported by annotation. The annotation often pairs words—both academic vocabulary and relevant supporting language—with color-coding, additions to a diagram (arrows, circling, and so on) or easy labels to further support ELLs' language development.

Supporting English Language Learners When Using This Routine

- Use sentence starters and sentence frames to develop structural language (e.g., chunk, change, connect) and help students communicate structural elements of representations.
- Make use of the Four Rs to provide multiple opportunities to develop and refine academic language crucial for describing structural connections among representations.
- Ensure that gestures and annotation support the structural ideas and language and thinking that is being communicated verbally.

Connecting Representations in Action

The following vignette provides an illustration of the Connecting Representations routine, focusing on excerpts at key points where there are supports for students with learning disabilities as well as supports for ELLs.

To focus on these supports, the vignette portrays a classroom that is already starting to be familiar with the routine. This is the fourth time the students have used the routine, so they now understand the flow of the routine and are beginning to be able to highlight structural connections through annotation. (For more information on how to first introduce the routine to students, see Chapter 7. For additional suggestions for math tasks to use in this routine, see Appendix D.)

Classroom Snapshot: Mr. Smith's Eighth-Grade Math Class

Mr. Smith teaches both sixth and eighth grade in his school. Having tried the routine with his sixth graders, he has also been starting to use it in his eighth-grade class. The urban district in which Mr. Smith teaches is quite diverse, and his class has nearly 50 percent English learners with three different first languages. In addition, five students in the class have an Individualized Education Program (IEP). You will meet a subset of these students in the vignette, including:

- Katy and Jacob who have IEPs:
  - Katy struggles with working memory and demonstrates strong visual-spatial processing skills. Supports in her IEP include use of graphic organizers and reference sheets.
  - Jacob struggles with attention and organization and is a strong verbal processor. Supports in his IEP include regular refocusing cues and movement breaks.
- The ELLs include Fatima, Samira, Omar, Carlos, and Jayden.
  - Samira has only been in the school for one month. She speaks Arabic and very little English. Mr. Smith has seated her next to Fatima, a former limited English proficient student who also speaks Arabic. Omar is another Arabic speaker who most recently was assessed at an English language development proficiency level 4.
  - Jayden entered the class at an English language development proficiency level 2, though Mr. Smith suspects his English proficiency is higher, at least in terms of speaking. Cape Verdean Creole is spoken at home.
  - Even though Carlos is designated as a "former limited English proficient student," Mr. Smith continues to provide academic language production support, especially writing support. Spanish is spoken at home.

Because of the large number of ELLs in his classes, Mr. Smith often uses the Connecting Representations routine because as he thinks it's a great way to build language; as he says, "It gives students something to talk about." The receptive nature of the first part of the routine also downplays Katy's working memory issues, and including visual representations plays to her visual-spatial processing strength. The pairing and sharing play to Jacob's verbal processing strength, and the annotation helps focus his attention. Mr. Smith also finds that the annotation helps the English learners follow the conversation. Finally, Mr. Smith uses the way students share their connections with a partner in the full group—one pointing and one speaking—

to encourage some of his beginning English speakers to participate in full-group discussion.

CHOOSING HIS REPRESENTATIONS

The class is about to embark on the functions unit and Mr. Smith wants to see what his students remember from their work with slope and rate of change from seventh grade. He also wants to see if any of his students have the misconception that a graph is a picture. He has chosen to have students connect a set of distance–time graphs and written stories (Figure 4.10). He wonders which features of graphs stu-

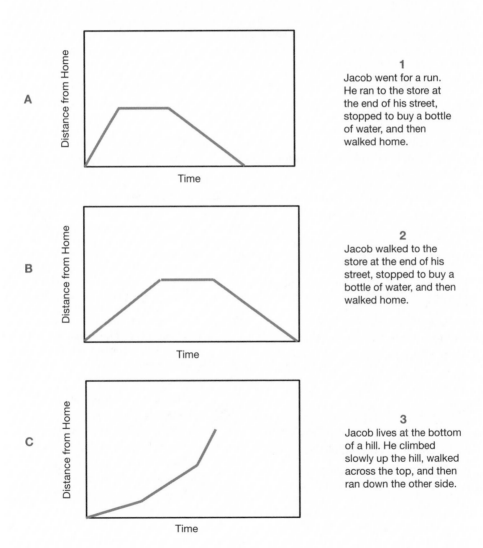

1
Jacob went for a run. He ran to the store at the end of his street, stopped to buy a bottle of water, and then walked home.

2
Jacob walked to the store at the end of his street, stopped to buy a bottle of water, and then walked home.

3
Jacob lives at the bottom of a hill. He climbed slowly up the hill, walked across the top, and then ran down the other side.

Figure 4.10

dents will notice, and the extent to which they will describe those features in terms of a relationship between the two quantities (distance and time). He has deliberately chosen a "hill" context (adapted from Shell Center 2015) to see if some students will fall into the trap of matching it with a graph that looks like a hill. These are also new kinds of representations for the routine, and Mr. Smith is curious to see if the students will chunk the graphs and descriptions, as they have started to do with algebraic expressions and shapes.

Mr. Smith chose to omit Graph C and have students create that missing representation because he thought it would surface the graph as a picture misconception if any of his students had it. Additionally, he thought writing a story would be a stretch for his English learners at this point, and they would be better able to demonstrate their thinking if they were creating a graph.

PART 1: LAUNCH

In Part 1 of the routine, the teacher orients students to the structural thinking they are about to engage in, provides the flow of the activity, and gives students an opportunity to enter the problem.

Mr. Smith launches the Connecting Representations routine by briefly revisiting the purpose and flow of the routine, and introduces his thinking goal for the lesson:

> *Today we practice thinking like mathematicians by connecting two things that look different. The two representations we will connect are graphs and words.*

To support his ELLs and help his students focus, he projects the goal and steps of the routine. He will do this throughout the other parts of the routine as well.

PART 2: INTERPRET AND CONNECT REPRESENTATIONS

Part 2 of the routine provides students with multiple passes and contexts in which to notice features of and make connections between representations, on their own, with a partner, and in the full group. Annotation is used to highlight and sentence stems and frames are used to focus student attention on the common structure underneath the matching pairs of representations.

Mr. Smith directs student attention to two pieces of newsprint that are folded and tacked up on the front board. He unfolds the first to reveal three short stories (Figure 4.11). He numbers each story and writes *story*

STORY

1. Jacob went for a run. He ran to the store at the end of his street, stopped to buy a bottle of water, and then walked home.

2. Jacob walked to the store at the end of his street, stopped to buy a bottle of water, and then walked home.

3. Jacob lives at the bottom of a hill. He climbed slowly up the hill, walked across the top, and then ran down the other side.

Figure 4.11

at the top of the newsprint. He then asks three students to read the stories aloud to the class. While each student reads, Mr. Smith "acts out" the story. He explains that in a minute he will unveil the second piece of newsprint showing two graphs. He projects and then gives individual think time instructions.

Individual Think Time

> **Mr. Smith:** One minute of quiet think time. Ask yourself, "What part of the story will help me connect to the graph?" "What part of the graph will help me connect to the story?"

Mr. Smith unveils the graphs, labels each, and titles the newsprint "graph" (Figure 4.12). He watches as students stare silently at the newsprint, their eyes moving back and forth periodically between graph and story. As he watches he notices some students tracing parts of the graph in the air with their finger. *Could they be visually chunking the graph?* he wonders.

Pairs

Mr. Smith projects the following three sentence frames, stands next to them, and then calls the class back together.

> I noticed _____.
>
> An important part of the graph is _____.
>
> An important part of the story is _____.

Mr. Smith: Time to share with your partner what you are noticing about the parts of the graphs and stories and how those parts are helping you connect or match a story and a graph. (*Pointing to the sentence frames*) Use these sentence frames when you share what you noticed or saw in the graph or story that you think would help you connect two representations. Use what you are noticing to match a story with a graph.

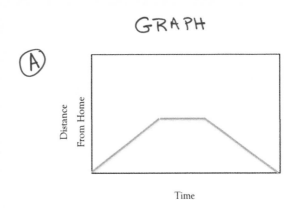
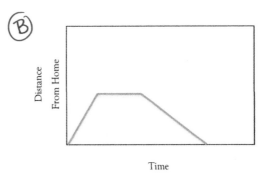

GRAPH

Figure 4.12

Mr. Smith watches as students turn to their tablemates and start talking. Careful not to stand between students and the posted graphs and stories, he quickly tours the room, listening in on student conversations. He is listening for evidence that students are breaking the graphs and stories into pieces and connecting those chunks based on speed and that they are keying in on distance away from the house versus time.

As he walks around the room, he places one copy of a handout with the two graphs on Jacob's table to help him focus, on Jayden's table to help him communicate his thinking with Nick, and on Samira's table thinking it may help him "see" her thinking. He lingers, listening in as Jayden and Nick talk.

Jayden: An important part of the graph is this line across (*Pointing to the horizontal pieces of both graphs*).

Nick: Yeah, that's when he's at the store. (*Jayden looks quizzically at Nick and Nick continues.*) He stops. He's not going anywhere so the graph is flat.

Jayden (*Looking up at the posted stories*): He stopped in one. And two (*Pointing in the direction of the posted stories*). He ran, stopped, and walked in one. In two he (*Pauses*) walked (*Pauses*) the same (*Pointing to the first and last chunk of Graph A*). This lines are the same. Two is Graph A.

Nick: Then the other graph goes with the first story.

Mr. Smith: It sounds like you two have matched both graphs. I'd like you to share your match for Graph A with the class. Remember how we do this in Connecting Representations?

Nick: A speaker and a pointer.

Mr. Smith: Right. Nick, why don't you speak, and Jayden, you point. Take the next couple minutes to rehearse. Nick, work on slowly and clearly explaining what you two noticed that helped you find the match. Jayden, listen carefully and practice pointing to the parts of the graph or story as Nick is talking about them. (•)

Mr. Smith moves over near Jacob and Carlos. As he walks past Fatima and Samira, he hears them talking animatedly in Arabic. He pauses and looks more closely. Samira's left index finger is halfway up the y-axis in line with the horizontal segment of Graph A. Her right finger is sliding back and forth along the x-axis underneath the horizontal segment of the graph. He thinks maybe Samira and Fatima are focusing in on the relationships between time and distance as they make sense of the graph.

Mr. Smith shifts position and listens in on Jacob and Carlos.

Jacob: It has to be one because I run to the store and walk back.

Carlos: The line is like (*Running his finger up and down the first segment of Graph B*), more, it's more up than this (*Now moving his finger to the last segment of Graph B*). So one goes with this one.

(•) Mr. Smith decided to have Jayden and Nick share their thinking in the full group because they were keying in on chunks of the graphs and the story and had identified a key feature of a graph (i.e., a horizontal line) and connected it to stopping at the store. He gives them time to prepare their presentation roles. This is especially important for Jayden so that he can practice listening to the way Nick explains their thinking and then connecting the words to the appropriate parts of the graph and story. Additionally, preparing to present gives the boys something productive to do while other pairs in the room continue making connections.

Jacob: Yeah, I get to the store faster. And here (*Moving his figure along the last segment in Graph B*) is when I'm walking home. See, it's slower.

Carlos: 'Cause you outta shape, bro. (*Carlos hits Jacob in the shoulder and the two boys laugh.*)

Carlos and Jacob start to drift off task. Mr. Smith quickly scans the room. He sees that three pairs have stopped talking. He decides he better pull the group back together. ⊙

Share and Discuss ⊙

Mr. Smith projects and reminds students of the structure for sharing connections in the full group: Partners will come to the front of the room to present together; then one student will talk and the other will point to the aspect of the graph or story that is being explained. The class is to watch and listen carefully. Mr. Smith tells students to use the sentence frames in Figure 4.13 when sharing their thinking.

Presenter	Audience
We noticed _____ so we _____.	They noticed _____ so they _____.
We knew _____ so we _____.	They knew _____ so they _____.
Our connection makes sense because _____.	Their connection makes sense because _____.

Figure 4.13

Mr. Smith: Jayden, Nick, come up to the front of the room and share the connection you made with the class. Jayden, why don't you stand right there between the graphs and stories. Nick, stand off to the side. Please start with what you and Jayden noticed (*Pointing to the first sentence frame*). Everyone listen to Nick and watch what Jayden is pointing to. Think about what they noticed, and what they did.

Nick: Jayden noticed that both graphs had a flat spot in the middle. (*Jayden points to the horizontal segments on Graph A and B.*) So we thought that was when Jacob was at the store 'cause he wasn't going anywhere. But then he stopped at the store in both stories. (*Jayden points in the general direction of the first and second story.*) But in the second one, he walks to the store and he walks home from the store so we picked Graph A because it was the same.

⊙ Do not wait until all students in the room have stopped discussing the task to stop partner work. Transition to group work when you start to see signs of pairs finishing up. The discussion will continue in the full group.

⊙ Providing students who struggle with language or attention with a copy of the visual that they can point to while they work helps provide access and supports communication between partners. It also provides the teacher with a window into student thinking. For example, although Mr. Smith did not understand what Samira and Fatima were saying, by watching where Samira was placing her finger on the paper, he could see that they were focusing in on the quantities represented by both axes and connecting them to the graph. If the girls were merely pointing "in the air" at the graphs posted in the front of the room, he would not know what they were talking about.

(*Jayden points to the first and last segments of Graph A.*) In the second graph, the first and last parts are different, one's steeper than the other.

Mr. Smith (*Addressing the class*): What did Jayden and Nick notice that helped them connect Graph A to the second story? Use the sentence frame (*Pointing in the direction of the projected frames*). "They noticed _____ so they _____." Katy?

Katy: They noticed the flat part so they looked for a part in the story when he wasn't moving. They also noticed that the other two parts of the graph were the same and he walked to and from the store in the second story so they connected the first graph to the second story.

Mr. Smith: OK, so Nick and Jayden noticed one part or chunk of the graph that was flat. Jayden, can you point to the chunk? (*Jayden points.*) And what part or chunk of the story did they connect to the flat or horizontal chunk of the graph?

Malcom: Stopping at the store to buy water.

Mr. Smith walks over to the stories, picks up a blue marker, then circles the word *stopped*, and underlines the clause "stopped to buy a bottle of water" in the second story. He then hands the blue marker to Jayden and, gesturing a circle, asks him to circle the horizontal chunk of Graph A.

Mr. Smith: What else did Katy say they noticed?

Katy: They noticed that the other two parts of the graph were the same.

Mr. Smith (*Tossing a green marker to Jayden*): Jayden, can you circle (*Gesturing*) the other two chunks of Graph A with green marker. (*Waiting for Jayden to annotate the graph*) Katy, what parts or chunks of the second story did they connect to the two chunks of the graph Jayden just circled in green?

Katy: Walking to the store and walking home.

Mr. Smith: Nick, can you annotate those two chunks of the story with the green marker? Just like I did with the blue—circle *walked* and underline the clause.

Jayden hands the green marker to Nick and Nick annotates the second story. Mr. Smith thanks Jayden and Nick and asks them to take their seats. He then draws the class's attention to the annotated connection.

Mr. Smith: Take a look at Graph A and the second story. Nick and Jayden connected these two representations by breaking the graph up into chunks (*He points to the green, blue, and green chunks*) and connecting them to the chunks of the story (*He points to the green, blue, and green chunks in the second story B*). ⚀ ⚁

⚀ Mr. Smith underscores this idea of chunking in structural thinking. He uses color to highlight the chunks of the graph and connect them to the matching chunk of the story. The annotation also helps students who struggle with understanding and staying focused on the full group discussion.

⚁ Notice that Mr. Smith is starting to hand over some of the annotation to the students. The first few times they did the routine, Mr. Smith did all the annotating. This time he consciously models annotating the first connection and then invites Nick and Jayden to annotate the connection between the remaining chunks. Annotation is a tool that all students should have, and Mr. Smith is consciously developing it through the Connecting Representations routine.

Mr. Smith: Let's look at Graph B. Jacob, Carlos, would you please come up and tell us which story you connected the second graph to? Carlos, would you please do the speaking, and Jacob, would you please point? ⦿

(*Mr. Smith draws attention back to the projected roles and reminds Carlos to use the sentence frames.*)

Carlos: We knew that Jacob ran, then stopped, and then walked home. (*Jacob acts out running, stopping, and walking in place. The class laughs.*)

Carlos: So we looked for a graph with three different parts. B has three chunks. Jacob, show it. The first line is steep (*Jacob points*), then the flat stopping part like in A (*Jacob points*), and then the last walking part (*Jacob points*).

Mr. Smith: Who can repeat what Carlos said about how they connected Graph B? Omar?

Omar: They connected Graph B to the first story.

Mr. Smith: And, how did they make the connection, Omar? What did they notice? Use one of these (*Pointing*) sentence frames. Jacob, as Omar rephrases, remember to point to help us see what he is saying.

Omar (*Looking at the sentence frames*): They knew that it was run, stop, walk (*Jacob points to the words in the first story*) so they looked for a graph with three different parts (*Jacob points to the three parts of the graph*). ⦿⦿

Mr. Smith (*Writing the word* steep *next to the graph*): Carlos said, "The first line is steep." How does the steepness of a line (*Gesturing by rotating his arm to show steepness*) help you connect it to an action in the story?

Katy: The steeper the line, the faster you are going. So running would be the steepest part.

(*Mr. Smith records* steeper *and* steepest *on the board too. He repeats each word, gesturing the three stages with his arm.*) ⦿⦿⦿

Mr. Smith thanks Carlos and Jacob and asks them to take their seats. As they do, he circles the words *ran*, *stopped*, and *walked* in the first story. (Figure 4.14.) Pointing to each word, he asks students to use this idea of steepness to connect each chunk of the graph with an action in the story. As they respond, he labels each part of the graph. (Figure 4.15.)

⦿ Having Jacob come up to the front of the room to present provides him with a movement break, something that his IEP suggests. In addition, assigning him the role of pointer will help Jacob to stay focused in the discussion. Assigning Carlos the speaking role puts him in a position to work on his language production.

⦿⦿ The audience sentence frames help students keep focused on the thinking of their classmates. They can also provide language support for restating or rephrasing another's idea.

⦿⦿⦿ Mr. Smith draws attention to a term (*steep*) that Carlos used to describe the running chunk of the graph. Steepness is an important aspect of a graph to attend to and he would like students to have more precise language to use when discussing it. He records the term (and its various forms), demonstrates the definition, and has a student connect the term to the underlying mathematics. The recorded terms will serve as a reference—for all students, but especially for the English learners—as the lesson continues and student math understanding and language become more precise.

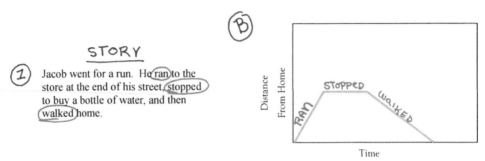

STORY

(1) Jacob went for a run. He (ran) to the store at the end of his street, (stopped) to buy a bottle of water, and then (walked) home.

Figure 4.14   Figure 4.15

PART 3: CREATE NEW REPRESENTATIONS

In Part 3 of the routine, students use what they have learned about important features of the connected representations to create the missing representation. They have time to think on their own before working with a partner to create a matching representation and discussing in the full group. The teacher uses annotation to highlight features of the representations and uses sentence stems and frames to focus students' attention on the common underlying structure.

Mr. Smith draws students' attention to the unmatched story (see Figure 4.11, story 3, on p. 90) and tells them that it's time to create the graph for this last story using what they have learned. He reminds them that they will use the familiar think-pair-share flow to create and discuss the missing representation. Then he reads the story (acting out the movements) and then projects and verbally gives the individual think time instructions.

Individual Think Time

Mr. Smith: One minute to think individually: What would the graph of this story look like? Ask yourself, *How is this story the same as the other stories? How is it different?*

(*As the students think, Mr. Smith quickly sketches an x- and y-axis on the board labeling them* time *and* distance from home, *respectively.*)

Pairs

Mr. Smith (*Bringing the class back together*): Now I'd like you to work with a partner to sketch a graph (*Pointing to the blank axes he's drawn*) that matches our last story. (*He projects and reads the pair work instructions.*) Start by sharing the parts of the story that you think tell you something about what the graph looks like. Use this sentence frame when you share: "The story says _____ so the graph will _____."

Mr. Smith wants his students to articulate their structural thinking using the sentence frames rather than immediately trying to find the "right answer" for the graph, so he waits until he hears the pairs start sharing and then hands out one piece of paper to each pair with a labeled x- and y-axis on which the students can sketch their graphs. He then tours the room, looking at the graphs students are sketching and listening in on their conversations. He is looking and listening for evidence that students are seeing the three chunks of the story and thinking about speed in terms of the steepness of the graph. He notes that students are seeing the chunks of the graph, but are grappling with how to sketch the relative steepness of each of those chunks. He also notes that no one appears to hold the misconception that the graph is a picture of the situation: no one is sketching the hill on their graph!

Share and Discuss

Mr. Smith: Fatima and Samira, would you please sketch your graph on the blank axis I've made on the front board? I don't want you to explain it, just reproduce it so everyone can think about it.

(Samira looks nervously at Fatima. They exchange a few words in Arabic and then both girls come to the front of the room. Fatima hands Samira the black marker, and Samira sketches the graph.) [See Figure 4.16.] 🔘

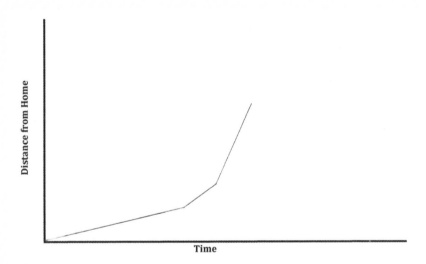

Figure 4.16

Individual Think Time and Pairs

Mr. Smith: Class, take a look at Samira and Fatima's graph. Take ten seconds of individual think time: Do you agree that their graph accurately represents

> 🔘 Students share the representations they created in the full group, but they do not explain their thinking to the group. This provides the class one more opportunity to make sense of and look for connections between two representations.

the story? (*He pauses for ten seconds.*) OK, turn and talk to your partner. Does this graph match the story? Be able to explain why or why not. (•)

Share and Discuss

Mr. Smith: Malcolm, what did you and Emily decide? Does Samira and Fatima's graph accurately represent the story?

Malcolm: Yes. This story is like the other two. It has three parts to it—climbing slowly, walking, and then running. You can see the three parts to their graph (*Gesturing with his arm*) slow, faster, fastest.

Mr. Smith: Who can repeat what Malcolm just said about connecting the three parts or chunks of the story to the steepness (*Gesturing*) of the graph?

Carlos: The first chunk of the graph is climbing slowly up the hill. (*Mr. Smith writes* climbing slowly *above the first chunk.*) The middle chunk is walking across the top. (*Mr. Smith labels the next chunk* walking.) The last chunk is running down the other side. (*Mr. Smith writes* running.)

(*Mr. Smith decides to end the discussion there and transitions the class to the last part of the routine, reflecting on their thinking.*)

See Chapter 7 for sample reflection prompts for the Connecting Representations routine.

> (•) Notice that Mr. Smith intentionally provides individual think time for students to make sense of the newly posted graph because this representation is one that students have not yet created or interpreted. He also allows students time to process the graph with their partners. This helps students solidify both their thinking and their language, better positioning them for the full group discussion.

Important Takeaways

Within the vignette you've just read, there are several important points we'd like to underscore about developing structural thinking through the routine. Think about how these relate to your own instruction as you use this routine:

- Highlighting connections between mathematical representations is one way to develop students' familiarity with looking for similarities in mathematical structure.

- Purposefully choosing representations helps students be successful. By choosing representations that both build from their learning strengths and give them practice with representations that provide some challenge, students can build their "math muscles" for seeing structure.

- The language of *chunk*, *change*, and *connect* allows students to articulate their thinking and captures three important actions that are part of structural thinking. Modeling the language, encouraging the use of it through sentence stems, and recording it will support and develop it in students.

In the next chapter, we'll introduce a routine to support our final avenue of thinking: repeated reasoning.

Recognizing Repetition

An Instructional Routine to Support Students' Repeated Reasoning

"**Can I show you** a couple of pieces of work my kids came up with earlier today?" Ms. Ramos asked Mr. Connors, one of her math colleagues. "We've been looking at visual patterns and trying to link generalized statements to the patterns to write an expression. But only a couple students were able to write a correct rule. I'm trying to think about what to do with the class to help them move away from just counting and guessing, or relying only on a recursive pattern like 'adding 3.'" Mr. Connors quickly scanned all the papers as they discussed them (see Figures 5.1 and 5.2).

Find a rule to determine the number of circles in any figure.

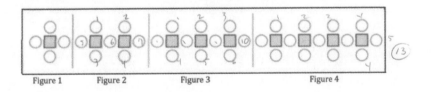

Figure #	1	2	3	4	10	100	N
# of Circles	4	7	10	13	31	103	n+3

Figure 5.1 Brianna's Work: In the table, Brianna appears to find correct values for Figures 1, 2, 3, 4, and 10 by successively adding 3 (she lists 16, 19, 22, 25, 28 next to 31). When she gets to 100, she appears to simply add $100 + 3$. Her rule, $n + 3$, is not correct.

Find a rule to determine the number of circles in any figure.

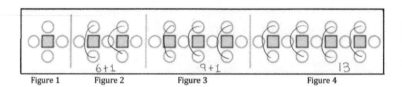

| Figure 1 | Figure 2 | Figure 3 | Figure 4 |

Figure #	1	2	3	4	10	100	N
# of Circles	4	7	10	13	30	300	3n

Figure 5.2 Larena's Work: In the table, Larena appears to find correct values for Figures 1, 2, 3, 4, but then appears to use a rule of multiplying the figure number by 3 to get 30 circles for figure 10 and 300 circles for figure 100. Her rule, $3n$, is not correct.

Ms. Ramos paused at Larena's work said, "And look at what's written under the figures: $6 + 1$, $9 + 1$, and the lines through the circles. It looks like she's counting the circles in groups of 3 and then adding that 1 last circle at the end each time. She's got it: $3n + 1$! But she just can't seem to turn that counting pattern into a rule." Ms. Ramos added, "It's as if once the students put numbers in a table, they don't think about the visual pattern anymore and how they counted, they just start looking for patterns in the table of numbers. How do I get them to pay attention to how they got the numbers in the first place? How do I get them to see that they can use *how* they counted as a way to help them generalize?"

The answer to the question Ms. Ramos is asking sits squarely in the repeated reasoning avenue of thinking: When mathematical thinkers approach a problem using repeated reasoning, they look for or create processes that repeat. They look for regularity in their counting, calculating, or constructing.

In this chapter, we'll explore what it means for students to reason through repetition and we'll introduce the instructional routine *Recognizing Repetition* to support all students' development of this avenue of thinking.

What Is "Repeated Reasoning"?

If you were able to watch students' thinking in slow motion as they used repeated reasoning, you would notice several different steps to that reasoning. These steps might happen more quickly or more slowly for different students, but all of them would occur in some form:

- **Pay attention to the process.** Students turn their attention to a *process* of counting, calculating, or constructing in their work, instead of just paying attention to the numbers, answers, or results.

- **Sense the regularity.** Students use their different senses to identify a pattern in the process. For example, some students will talk to themselves as they count, calculate, or build and listen to the rhythm in their words. Other students will pay attention to the "feel" of the pattern, as they move manipulatives in some repeated way. Other students will see some regularity in the figures in a visual pattern. Whatever senses come into play for students, they are using those senses to identify some regularity in the mathematical situation.

- **"Shortcut" the process.** If students have been recording their process, they can start to see some regularity in some of the steps and no longer need to work through each individual step. Certain parts of the process get consolidated into shorter steps; the "chunks" we talk about in Chapter 7 are starting to emerge.

- **Connect the process to an "input" value.** As students start to see these chunks emerging from the repetition, they need to connect their repeated process to some value that they know in the problem that can serve as an "input value." It's at this point that students start to shift from thinking about steps of an algorithm they're following to thinking about a relationship between sets of numbers, or a function. For example, in a problem like the one Larena and Brianna are doing, and in the Tower problem later in the vignette, the figure number becomes the input value. In Chapter 1, Roberto uses his guess as the input number. Connecting possible input numbers to their process allows students to move toward creating a rule.

- **Generalize the process to a rule.** Finally, they are able to generalize their process into a rule. This could be a rule stated in words only, or it might be a rule written symbolically.

Some Examples of Repeated Reasoning

When students are using the repeated reasoning avenue of thinking, they are paying attention to the regularity in the way they are counting, calculating, and constructing. They are looking for the "sameness" in their process as a clue for a more generalized process, and they are using different senses to notice that sameness. To see what we can learn about this, turn your attention from the numbers in the table to the notation students added around the pictures of the figures.

Brianna's Work: *Regularity in Counting*

In Brianna's work (Figure 5.3), the small numbers written near the figures provide a clue to how she was counting.

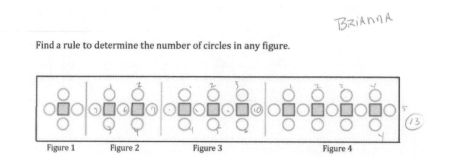

Find a rule to determine the number of circles in any figure.

Figure 1   Figure 2   Figure 3   Figure 4

Figure 5.3

From what she's written down within the figures, we can see that she had a system for counting the circles: she was paying attention to her process. Following her numbering, we could summarize her counting for Figure 2 as "top-top, bottom-bottom, middle-middle-middle." Figure 3 continues in this same manner: "top-top-top, bottom-bottom-bottom, middle-middle-middle-middle." Try reciting it out loud to yourself; you can already start to hear the rhythm in the repetition. Saying it and hearing it is one example of sensing the regularity. Notice how her numbering changes with each figure. We see:

- (for Figure 2) 1, 2, 3, 4, 5, 6, 7
- (for Figure 3) 1, 2, 3, 4, 5, 6 then in the rightmost circle, "10"
- (for Figure 4) 1, 2, 3, 4, then near the bottom circles, "4," then to the right of the middle circles, "5."

As she moves through the figures, she is starting to group some of the circles together. In Figure 4, instead of counting each circle, she counts the top ones, then groups the bottom ones together and writes 4, and groups the middle ones together and writes 5. Again, as she starts to see some regularity, there is less and less written residue of her thinking. An important next step in repeated reasoning happens when students begin to move from paying attention to each individual shape in a pattern or number in a calculation to consolidating part of the process—what we call "shortcutting" the process. This happens for Brianna when she does not need to count every single circle anymore, and adds 4 + 4 + 5 to get 13, circled to the right of Figure 4.

By practicing the routine, Brianna can become more adept at recognizing repetition in her reasoning and at connecting her process to a known "input" value like the figure number. Her work suggests that she is regularly counting "tops," then "bottoms," then "middles," and as she learns to notice this regularity, she can build from her counting to describe a pattern that relates to the figure number. In this case, she would learn to notice that the number of top circles matches the figure number, as does the number of bottom circles, and that the number of middle circles is one more than the figure number. She is well on her way to seeing that her counting pattern would result in the generalized expression $n + n + (n + 1)$, or maybe $2n + (n + 1)$, with $n =$ the figure number.

Larena's Work: *Regularity in Counting*

Larena's recording of her process suggests a different way of thinking about the regularity. In her work (Figure 5.4), her notation suggests that she was noticing:

Find a rule to determine the number of circles in any figure.

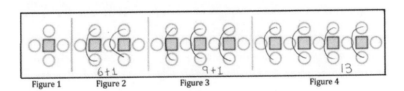

Figure 5.4

- (for Figure 2) Two groups of three circles with the rightmost one not included; she wrote 6 + 1

- (for Figure 3) Three groups of three circles with the rightmost one not included; she wrote 9 + 1

- (for Figure 4) Four groups of three circles with the rightmost one not included; she wrote 13.

Her work shows examples of repeated reasoning through her annotation, showing groups of three circles but writing her expression as a multiple of 3, + 1. Her teacher could help her see the repetition in her reasoning by pointing out her counting in Figure 2 as "3, 6, + 1 more." Then for Figure 3, "3, 6, 9, + 1 more." For Figure 4, "3, 6, 9, 12, + 1 more." Again, try reciting these out loud, or tracing them with your finger, as you say them; it underscores the rhythm in both the counting and the process of clustering the circles together. She has developed a system for counting the circles, used whatever senses she needs to notice the regularity, and has moved from writing 6 + 1, and 9 + 1, to 13, starting to shortcut her process.

We can see Larena moving into shortcutting by what she's written under each of the figures. Notice that she writes *6 + 1* in Figure 2, *9 + 1* in Figure 3, but then only writes *13* in Figure 4. This is evidence that she's starting to create a shortcut, moving from paying attention to individual elements of the process to clustering certain elements in a way that points toward a generalized process. With each figure, Larena leaves less and less written residue of her thinking.

Over time, as Larena learns to recognize repetition in her reasoning, she will be able to tell us that there are always groups of three with one left over on the end, but that the number of groups of three increases each time. From this, she will be able to create a generalized rule. In the way that Larena has noticed the regularity, the figure number matches the number of "arcs of three" that she's identified, and there is always one left over at the far right. Her generalized expression would be $3n + 1$.

An Overview of the Recognizing Repetition Routine

The Recognizing Repetition routine is designed to help students learn to focus on the regularity in their process of counting, calculating, or building, rather than on the results of that process. Although it's useful to pay attention to the results, those are "math muscles" that are already well developed; this routine is focused on building less well-developed "math muscles" for paying attention to processes, operations, and calculations.

The Steps of the Routine

The Recognizing Repetition routine has five parts. Recall from Chapter 2 that each routine begins with an initial introduction to the routine (Part 1), including sharing a mathematical thinking goal with your students, and ends with a student reflection on how they developed their mathematical thinking and how they might use it in future problems (Part 5).

Parts 2, 3, and 4 are unique to this routine. In this routine, students articulate regularities they notice in their process (Part 2) and then generalize that repetition (Part 3). They discuss the generalizations, making connections between their processes and a generalized rule (Part 4).

These next sections provide a brief overview of the five parts of the routine. Later, we provide a classroom illustration of what this routine looks like in action, and we'll highlight particular supports for special populations.

Part 1: Launch the Routine

When launching the routine, the teacher identifies the thinking goal for the routine and reviews the steps of the routine. It is critical that students understand that they are "recognizing repetition" to develop the habit of looking for regularity in their counting, calculating, and constructing. That is, that they are not working on this activity to get the answer to this one particular problem, but rather to develop a way of thinking mathematically that will help them find answers to any number of problems.

Steps for Part 1

1. Display and explain the thinking goal. For example, you might say, "Today we are going to learn how to think like mathematicians. We are going to use repetition in our reasoning to generalize a problem situation." (See Chapter 7 for examples of thinking goals you can use with this routine.)

2. Display and explain the flow and format of the routine. Help students understand that they will be looking for and describing ways in which they do the same steps over and over, generalizing those steps individually and with a partner, discussing their generalizations in the full group, and, finally, reflecting on their learning.

Part 2: *Notice Repetition*

In the second part of the Recognizing Repetition routine, students focus on identifying any regularities that they notice in their mathematical processes for making sense of the problem. Using a think-pair-share structure, students count, draw, build, calculate, or otherwise engage in a process and reflect on and discuss any regularities they are sensing in that process. Individual think time and an "ask-yourself" question are used to provide students time to engage in and hunt for repetition in their process. Students share how they are counting, constructing, or calculating and what about that process is the same each time with their partner. Then they share those regularities with the whole class as the teacher records the repetitions through specific annotation.

Steps for Part 2

Individual Think Time

1. Read the problem situation together, and set students off to engage in a process that will allow them to sense regularities. Help students orient to the repetition by having them ask themselves, "What do I keep doing the same each time?"

Pair

2. Have students share their process and any regularities they noticed with a partner.

Share and Discuss

3. First, ask students to describe their counting, constructing, or calculating process and say what about it was the same each time. Provide starters and frames like:

Every time I _____.

I always _____.

Annotate

4. Record the regularity in the various counting, constructing, or calculating processes.

Part 3: *Generalize Repetition*

The purpose of this next part of the routine is to help students work toward creating a generalization based on the repetition they have identified in their counting, constructing, or calculating process. They begin to think about a generalization on their own, then refine their thinking with a partner to produce a generalization together. Ask-yourself questions like "What were the steps in my process?," "What operations can I use to model this process?," and "Have I included every step?" help students abstract the process.

Steps for Part 3

Individual Think Time

1. Provide students individual think time to begin building a rule from the repetition they noticed in their process. Offer ask-yourself questions to provide support to focus students on the steps of their repeated process. Keep the individual think time short—enough time for students to generate some ideas and begin thinking about a rule, but not so much time that they have created the rule. The purpose of the individual think time is to get students ready to discuss their ideas about how to translate the repetition they discovered into a rule and then together with a partner create the actual rule.

Pair

2. Have students share how they started to think about generalizing.

3. After students share their initial ideas, have them work together to transform the repetition into a rule.

   While partners work:

   - Circulate and observe the range of rules in the room.

   - Consider how you will select and sequence roughly three generalizations for the full-group discussion.

Part 4: *Discuss Generalizations*

Finally, students have an opportunity to practice reading and interpreting other students' rules and connecting those rules to the regularity in another process. This helps students deepen their understanding of the meaning of mathematical notation.

During this part of the routine, the teacher posts a rule, then gives students a few seconds of individual think time to make sense of the rule. Students talk with a partner about how the rule relates to some generalized process, then they share their ideas in the full group. The discussion focuses on connections that students see between the counting, constructing, or calculating process and the generalized rule. Finally, students determine if the rule works for the problem. Throughout the discussion, the teacher is annotating the rule to highlight the connection to the underlying regularity in process.

Steps for Part 4

Individual Think Time

1. Select and post a generalization for the class to consider. Give students a few seconds of individual think time to interpret the rule. Ask questions like "What actions do these operations suggest?" and "What does the variable represent?"

Pair

2. Prompt students to talk with a partner about what repeated process the rule generalizes.

Share and Discuss

3. Ask one or two students who did not create the rule to discuss features of the rule (e.g., operations, variables, relationships, chunks, expressions, and so on) that clued them into the process it generalizes. Press students to determine if the generalization accurately captures the process, if it can be stated more precisely, and if the rule "works" (drawing on MP3 and MP6).

4. Annotate: As students share, annotate the rule to highlight how it connects to the process it generalizes.

Part 5: Reflect on Repeated Reasoning

In the last part of the routine, students reflect on what they have learned about repeated reasoning that will help them in their future problem solving and math learning. If time is running short, it is better to discuss one fewer rule and save time for the reflection than to skip or shortchange this opportunity to reflect on the avenue of thinking.

Steps for Part 5

Individual Write Time

1. Frame the reflection by revisiting the thinking goal for this routine. Provide students with sentence starters and frames to focus their reflection (e.g., "When looking for repetition in a process, I learned to pay attention to _____ because _____" or "One way to identify repetition is to _____"). Give students 1–3 minutes of quiet writing time to reflect and complete a sentence frame.

Pair

2. Have students share what they wrote with a partner. Listen in as partners share and select two or three ideas related to the thinking goal to be shared in the full group.

Share

3. Have two or three students share what they learned about identifying and generalizing regularity in repeated reasoning. Record the statements and post for future reference.

The entire routine-at-a-glance is shown in Figure 5.5. As you look at the routines across these chapters, note the parallels between the flows of each routine; this can help you become familiar with them more easily.

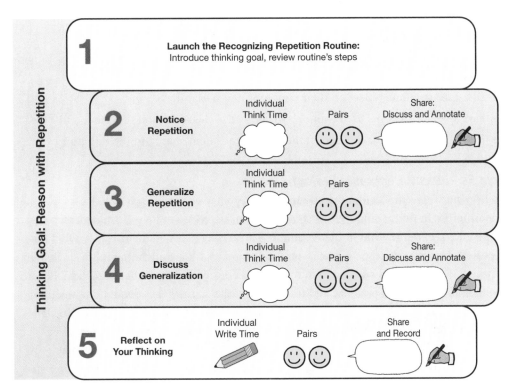

Figure 5.5

Essential Strategies in the Routine

Although all the essential strategies are involved in this routine, the essential strategies of ask-yourself questions and the Four Rs are particularly crucial for providing focus and access in this routine.

Essential Strategies

- Ask-yourself questions
- Annotation
- Sentence frames and sentence starters
- Four Rs: repeat, rephrase, reword, record

Ask-Yourself Questions

Because students are so well practiced at focusing on number patterns and looking for regularity in the objects of a pattern—the numbers, the shapes, and so on—it can be difficult to redirect attention to looking for regularity in their processes—their operations, their calculations, their problem-solving steps. The ask-yourself questions are written to keep the focus on their process, rather than their results.

Look for examples of these kinds of ask-yourself questions in particular during individual think time in:

- Part 2, as students reflect on their own repeated reasoning
- Part 3, when students are beginning to generalize the repetition they've found
- Part 4, when students are interpreting a generalization shared in the full group.

Four Rs: *Repeat, Rephrase, Reword, Record*

To help students learn to identify and focus on repeated reasoning, you can look for opportunities to repeat any cycle of steps a student describes to help all students hear (and sometimes see) the rhythm in the repetition. Rephrasing helps students clarify what the repeated steps are, so in some places, you may want to ask a student to rephrase what was repeated. Rewording allows you to introduce more formal mathematical language. Recording then helps students organize and track the process so they can identify the repetition, and particularly supports students who are strong visual-spatial thinkers. Recording language can also support language development through more precise rewording.

As we said in Chapter 2, the attention to the *rephrasing* and *rewording* steps may grow or shrink, depending on your needs in the lesson, sometimes omitting the *rewording* step altogether if it's not relevant. In the upcoming vignette, you'll see repeat-rephrase-record, without the need for rewording yet.

Look for examples of repeating, rephrasing, rewording, and/or recording in:

- Part 2, in whole-class sharing as students share their processes
- Part 4, in whole-class discussion as students discuss their generalizations.

Challenges, Opportunities, and Supports for Students with Specific Needs

Two important aspects that can serve as entry points to the thinking, particularly for special populations, are the use of their different senses to notice their own repeated reasoning and gradually consolidating that repetition into some kind of generalized form.

Students with Learning Disabilities

The final destination of the repeated reasoning avenue of thinking is often a rule or generalization, a tall order for many students with learning disabilities. This challenge is intensified for a student who also struggles with organization, because students can more easily identify their own repeated reasoning when they have an organized approach and are methodically recording their steps. Students with learning disabilities can use an area of strength to help them identify the repetition in their thinking. Students who are strong visual-spatial thinkers can use that strength to look for repetition in the way they are drawing or building. Students who are strong verbal or auditory processors can count out loud or describe the way they counted to a partner, or listen to their partner talk through the process they are using. Kinesthetic learners can build. Having students begin by physically counting or constructing with manipulatives grounds the repeated reasoning in a concrete experience that can be mined for repetition not in seemingly disconnected numbers in a table.

Support for developing repeated reasoning is built in when students are asked to re-create the initial elements of a pattern, such as drawing or building the first few figures of a visual pattern, and when they are asked to count, show their partner how they counted, share their counting process with the full group, or revisit their counting process to consolidate the steps and generalize. It is built in when students explain their process to a partner as well as listen and watch as their partner shares his or her process. It is built in when teachers and students record and annotate the process.

Supporting Students with Learning Disabilities When Using This Routine

- Provide students a multitude of entry points by offering and encouraging a range of options for engaging in the process. For example, encourage students to—and let them decide whether they want to—redraw a pattern using colors, rebuild a pattern using manipulatives, recite steps of their process to themselves out loud, and so on.

- Continually draw students' attention to the regularity in their counting, constructing and calculating.

- Review, record, and annotate the students' counting, constructing, and calculating processes during discussions.

- Provide physical space to engage in the process (e.g., a table to build on) and a place to record the process (e.g., handout with figures to annotate, space to record a process, a "middle column" in a table to record steps, and so on) to help them organize what they notice about their process.

English Language Learners

Of the three avenues of thinking, repeated reasoning presents the fewest challenges for English language learners (ELLs). Most English learners are well practiced at looking for patterns in process: recognizing repetition in a new situation is a survival skill for a new-comer. Patterns and regularities help ELLs navigate through the new structures of their school day as they continuously make sense of the unfamiliar symbols they are seeing, sounds they are hearing, and ways of being in a foreign school and culture. Unable yet to interpret teacher instructions, ELLs watch the repeated actions of their English-speaking classmates. This habit of looking for and making sense of repetition and routine in an English language school day positions them well to developing repeated reasoning through the Recognizing Repetition routine, perhaps even giving them an advantage over their English-speaking peers.

English learners do not need command of the English language to communicate the repetition in their process: they can communicate the mathematical regularity they see through demonstrating and annotating their counting, calculating, or constructing process. Even if ELLs describe the repetition in their process using their first language, native English speakers can still identify the regularity as they can hear the rhythm in the tones and phrasing of the spoken language. Likewise, ELLs will be able to see the regularity in the processes other students enact and hear the rhythm in the verbal explanations of process, even if they do not fully understand the exact meaning of the words being said. Repeated reasoning is in many ways "mathematical music," and the rhythm can be heard regardless of the instrument used to create that music.

Although ELLs don't need to rely on English to have success with this routine, the routine is a powerful context in which to further develop language, because ELLs have something to talk about—their repeating process. Recreating their process is not cognitively demanding so their "brain space" can be freed up to work on the language to explain their actions. And, the descriptive language itself is repetitive. Language is developed through multiple think-pair-share cycles where the teacher models critical words and phrases and records them for all to see. It's developed through practice with a partner, through speaking in the full group, and finally through writing in the meta-reflection.

Supporting English Language Learners When Using This Routine

- Make the process visible through multiple opportunities to demonstrate with "voice-over," narrating the process as you do it.

- Include words and symbols when annotating the repetition so that ELLs develop language that's useful for articulating repetition.

- Craft sentence starters and frames that develop repeated reasoning language.

- Encourage them to use their first language to express themselves to increase their participation in the discussion.

Recognizing Repetition in Action

The following vignette provides an illustration of the Recognizing Repetition routine, focusing on excerpts at key points where there are supports for students with learning disabilities as well as supports for ELLs.

This is the second time the students have used the routine; they are just starting to understand the flow of the routine and what it means to focus on repetition in process. Ms. Ramos has talked with the students about learning to "think like mathematicians" and how the Recognizing Repetition routine will help them to develop the habit of looking for and generalizing repetition in their counting, calculating, and constructing processes. (For more information on how to first introduce the routine to students, see Chapter 7. For additional suggestions for math tasks to use in this routine, see Appendix E.)

Classroom Snapshot: Ms. Ramos' Seventh-Grade Math Class

Ms. Ramos was most concerned for these students:

- Alexa, Brianna, and Charlie all have an Individualized Education Program (IEP) that indicates weak conceptual processing. Their individualized plans call for working with concrete manipulatives and providing lots of examples. When the math gets abstract, these students struggle, but they have notable strengths, too:
  - Alexa and Brianna are very strong visual-spatial processors.
  - Charlie has strong verbal processing skills.
- Larena, Miguel, and Blanca are English learners at an English language development proficiency level 3 or 4.
  - Larena is a particularly strong math student, comfortable with numbers, quick to pick up procedures and visual-spatially strong.
  - All three have recently been pushed to participate actively in full-group discussions.
- Mateo and Cristian are recent arrivals to the school this year at about an English language development proficiency level 1. They talk with each other and Miguel in Spanish during group work, but neither has spoken in the full group yet.

Ms. Ramos thought that the repeated reasoning avenue of thinking would play to these students' strengths and help them build the capacity to generalize.

PART 1: LAUNCH

The class had been working on using algebraic expressions and equations to solve math problems. Students were struggling to use variables to represent quantities in a math problem and to construct simple equations. Ms. Ramos started using the Recognizing Repetition routine to help students develop the habit of looking for and generalizing repetition in a process. She chose the Towers task (Figure 5.6) because she wanted to ensure that Alexa, Brianna, and Charlie had a concrete way to sense a repeating process, and constructing towers with blocks provided that opportunity. In addition, the building process would help make Mateo's and Cristian's thinking more visible.

Towers

How many blocks will be in Tower 10? Tower 100? Tower *N*?

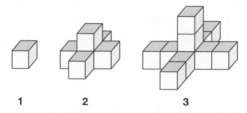

1   2   3

Figure 5.6 This task is inspired by Pattern #46 on the Visual Patterns website, www.visualpatterns .org/41-60.html.

Ms. Ramos launches the Recognizing Repetition routine by briefly revisiting the purpose and flow of the routine and introduces her thinking goal for the lesson: "Today we are going to learn to think like mathematicians by looking for repetition in how we build and count, to notice when our building and counting is the same each time." (See Figure 5.7.)

She ensures that students understand what repetition is by modeling it in her speech. She defines *recognize* by providing synonyms and prompting students to talk about how one recognizes repetition. To support her ELLs, she projects the words and provides gestures to accompany student explanations and her directions.

Recognizing Repetition	Notice Repetition	**?**
Think like a mathematician! *Look for repetition in your building and counting*	Generalize the Repetition	☺ ☺
	Discuss Generalizations	💬
	Reflect on Learning	✏

Figure 5.7

Part 2 of the routine provides students with multiple passes at focusing on a process and noticing repetition in their own building when they share their building processes in pairs, and when building processes are modeled, explained, recorded, and annotated in the full group. This combination of multiple passes with multiple modalities ensures students receive adequate processing opportunities.

Ms. Ramos projects the Towers task (Figure 5.8), gives the instructions, and places a container of 1-inch wooden cubes on each table for building.

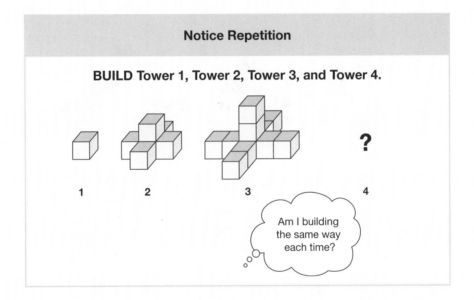

Figure 5.8

Individual Think Time

Ms. Ramos: Take a few minutes for some silent, individual thinking time. Your job is to notice repetition in the way you build the tower pattern. (*Holding up a container of blocks*) Individually, with these cubes, build Tower 1 (*Points to Tower 1*) Tower 2 (*Points to Tower 2*), Tower 3 (*Points to Tower 3*), and Tower 4 (*Points to the 4 and then the question mark*). As you build, remember to think like a mathematician (*Pointing to the thought bubble*) and ask yourself, *Am I building the same way each time?*

Students spill out the blocks and begin building towers. Ms. Ramos circulates, watching how students are building the towers. She looks to see if they are building in an organized fashion and if their building process is regular.

Ms. Ramos watches as Josh builds the towers by randomly setting the cubes into place. There doesn't seem to be any rhyme or reason to his building yet.

Ms. Ramos: Josh, it looks like you are building differently every time. Remember to ask yourself, *Am I building the same way each time?*

She watches as Alexa builds Tower 2. Alexa places five cubes down for the base of the tower (Figure 5.9) and then places one cube on top, in the center (Figure 5.10). When she builds Tower 3, she starts with the same five-cube base. This time she adds two cubes on top in the center and one cube next to each of the four "legs" (Figure 5.11). She constructs Tower 4 in the same way: placing five cubes down, adding three to the top center, and two cubes next to each of the four legs (Figure 5.12). Ms. Ramos wonders whether Alexa herself has noticed the regularity that she could so clearly see in Alexa's building process.

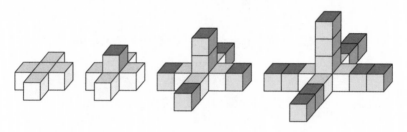

Figure 5.9   Figure 5.10   Figure 5.11   Figure 5.12

Ms. Ramos moves near Brianna's table to watch her build. Brianna starts by building the center stack (Figure 5.13). She then adds a cube in front and then a cube to the right. She very carefully reaches around the center stack to add a cube in the back and then places a cube to the left. She builds the next tower in the same manner, starting with the center stack and adding on a row of two cubes this time in each direction: front, right, back, and left. There is clearly regularity to Brianna's building process.

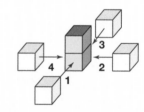

Figure 5.13

Ms. Ramos turns and catches Mateo building Tower 3. Mateo places three cubes down in a row. He then places two cubes in front, two cubes to the right, two cubes behind, and finally places two cubes on top (Figure 5.14). In her head, Ms. Ramos mentally records Mateo's Tower 3 building process as $3 + 2 + 2 + 2 + 2$, and wonders if he will build Tower 4 using the same process—doing $4 + 3 + 3 + 3 + 3$. Ms. Ramos watches as Mateo places four cubes down in a row, then places three cubes in front, three blocks to the right, three cubes behind, and three cubes on top.

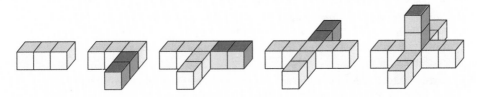

Figure 5.14

As Ms. Ramos walks to the front of the room to transition the class to partner work, she smiles to herself: every student is actively engaged in building towers and she watched as at least three of her struggling students—Alexa, Brianna, and Mateo—slipped into a regular building process. She wonders if they noticed the regularity in the way they are constructing towers. She will find out during the next part of the routine! ⊙

Pairs

The partner share provides students with another opportunity to recognize repetition and begin to describe the repetition they notice in their and their partner's building process. It provides additional processing time and adds a new modality—auditory processing—into the mix. The teacher's role is threefold: to ensure that students share their building process with their partner; to listen and look for evidence that students are noticing the regularity in their building processes; and to think about which students should share what repetition in the full group. As with individual think time, this partner work is not a time for the teacher to instruct.

Ms. Ramos projects instructions and begins.

> **Ms. Ramos** (*Pointing to the projected instructions*): Was there repetition in your building? Did you build in the same way each time? Show or explain how you built the towers to your partner. Partners, look and listen for repetition in the building.
>
> (*Ms. Ramos circulates, listening in on student conversation for evidence of repetition in the building processes of her students, and for clues that the students have recognized the repetition, e.g., are they using language like* same *and* every time *and* I just kept _____? *Curious to see if Alexa recognized the repetition she heads first over to Alexa and Laurie to listen to them sharing their construction processes.*)

⊙ Note that with the exception of Josh, Ms. Ramos did not interact with students as they were building the series of towers. The purpose of the individual think time is for students to engage in a process—in this case constructing—and sense any regularity in their process. This is not a time for the teacher to talk with students or question them about what they are doing. Ms. Ramos did stop and quickly remind Josh of the ask-yourself question, but she did not get into a conversation with him. Her purpose was not to show or teach Josh how to build a tower, but to encourage him to approach his building in a regular way.

Alexa: This is what I did. For 1, I just put a block. For the next one, I made the bottom (*Places five cubes down*) then I put one on top. For 3, I made the bottom, then I put a cube on each side like this, and two on the top. For the last one, it was the same. I made the bottom, put two cubes on each side and three cubes on the top.

Laurie: Mine was kind of the same. I just put one block for the first one. For Tower 2, I put one down, then I put four around it and one on top like this. For Tower 3, I put one down, then two cubes around it and two on top. Tower 4 would be one down, three cubes around it and three on top. ⊡

Ms. Ramos moves over to the table where Mateo, Miguel, and Cristian are sitting and watches. Mateo is pointing to his towers and speaking in Spanish to his tablemates.

Mateo (*Lifting up the top cube on Tower 2 and pointing to the cube under it and the leftmost cube*): Dos bloques. Uno, uno, uno. [See Figure 5.15.] (*Then placing the cube back down*) Uno. [See Figure 5.16.] (*Lifting the two cubes on top of Tower 3 he continues*) Tres bloques. Dos, dos, dos (*Pausing to place the two cubes back down*), dos. Torre cuatro. (*Lifting up three cubes on top of Tower 4*) Cuatro bloques, tres, tres, tres (*Pausing to place the three cubes back down*) tres.

Not only could she see the regularity in his building, but listening to Mateo explain his process, Ms. Ramos could clearly hear the regularity in Mateo's phrasing. And she was pretty sure the rest of the class could too. Now if she could only get Mateo to present to the full class, something he had not yet done. ⊡

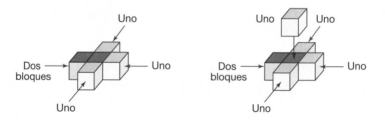

Figure 5.15   **Figure 5.16**

⊡ Hearing Alexa say that building the last tower "was the same" as building the previous towers is an indication that Alexa has recognized repetition in her building process. However, be careful that you do not fall into the trap of listening only for keywords to indicate repetition, such as *same*. For example, Laurie tells Alexa "Mine was kind of the same." In this case, the word *same* is referring to a commonality in the way she and Alexa went about building their towers, not saying that she is building towers in the same way each time, which would be an indication of repeated reasoning.

⊡ Asking students to share their building process with a partner provides them another opportunity and another modality through which to notice any regularity in their building process. The partner work also provides students with an opportunity to watch and listen for regularity in someone else's process. If a student's constructing was not regular, the partner share provides an opportunity for them to notice regularity in their partner's building process.

Share: Discuss and Annotate ⊙

Ms. Ramos pulls the students back together to share their building processes in the full group and identify regularities in those processes. She projects the slide (see Figure 5.17), and begins.

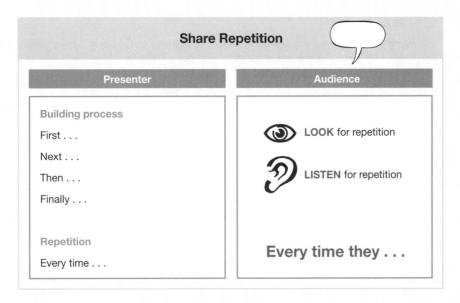

Figure 5.17

Ms. Ramos goes over the directions, pointing to the corresponding part of the directions on the slide as she does so, to help all her students understand what to pay attention to as other students share their process. She asks Brianna to share first.

Brianna (*Placing the cubes down as she explains*): OK, so one for the first tower. Then for the second tower, first I did the middle part, then a cube in front, a cube on the right, one in the back, and one on the left. For the next tower, I did the middle part, then two cubes in front, two cubes on the right, two in the back, and two on the left. The fourth would be the middle stack: three cubes in front, three on the right, three in back, and three left.

Ms. Ramos: Raise your hand if you saw or heard repetition in Brianna's building process. (*Almost all hands go up.*) Charlie?

⊙ Often, a whole-class sharing can turn into a single-modality event, with students and teacher using speaking as the main (only) means of communicating. Ms. Ramos tries to avoid this by intentionally bringing in other modalities, having students build for the class. In addition, she records students' building processes and annotates the towers. In doing so, she is not only providing multiple access points for a range of learners, she is also highlighting and capturing the repeated reasoning. Through the building, students with visual-spatial processing strengths like Brianna and Alexa are part of the conversation. Strong auditory processors like Charlie also have a way in.

Charlie: I heard it!

Ms. Ramos: What was the repetition you heard?

Ms. Ramos moves closer to the board to record the repetition as Charlie explains.

Charlie: First, she did the middle part, then cubes in front, then cubes on the right, then cubes in the back, and finally cubes on the left. Every time it was the middle part, then cubes in front, then on the right, then in the back, and lastly on the left.

Ms. Ramos: A very clear explanation Charlie. (*Pointing to the slide*) I especially liked how you used the sequencing language—first, then, finally—when you restated the repetition you heard in Brianna's building process.

Ms. Ramos: I saw Mateo showing Cristian and Miguel another way to build the towers. Mateo, please show us (*Gesturing to building*) your building process.

Mateo looks nervously at Miguel. They exchange a few words in Spanish. Mateo looks equal parts eager and anxious.

Ms. Ramos (*With an encouraging smile*): En español. (*Then to the class*) Watch carefully and listen carefully as Mateo builds. See if you can recognize the repetition in his building process. Make sure you can see Mateo's towers. ⊙

Mateo (*Pointing to the first tower*): Uno. (*Mateo lifts up the top cube on Tower 2 and points to the cubes underneath*) Dos bloques. (*He points to the front, right, and back cube, and says*) Uno, uno, uno (*Placing the cube back down*), uno. (*He lifts up the two cubes on top of Tower 3, motions to the blocks underneath*) Tres bloques. (*Pointing to the front, right, and back arms of the tower, he continues*) Dos, dos, dos (*Placing the two cubes back down*), dos. (*He continues in the same way*) Torre cuatro. (*Lifting up three cubes on top of Tower 4*) Cuatro bloques, tres, tres, tres (*Pausing to place the three cubes back down*), tres.

Ms. Ramos: Muy bueno. Who recognized the repetition in Mateo's building? What did Mateo do every time? (*Again, lots of hands*) Josh?

Josh: It was like, every time he would say one number like *dos* and then say like three more numbers and then a number. I can't remember exactly, but it was like, "Dos (*Pause*), tres, tres, tres (*Pause*), tres." Kind of like that. There was like a beat to it.

Ms. Ramos: So you heard a beat or rhythm in Mateo's words?

Josh: Yeah.

Ms. Ramos: Who else heard rhythm in or repetition in Mateo's words? Blanca? What repetition did you hear?

⊙ Ms. Ramos prompts Mateo to share his building process in his first language because Mateo has a repetition in his building process that she wants the class to hear, and being able to use Spanish provides a level of comfort that encourages him to take the risk of sharing. And because Ms. Ramos heard the rhythm when Mateo was describing his process to his tablemates in Spanish, she thought the other students might also be able to, and this would allow her to highlight the idea that rhythm can cue you into regularity in a process.

Blanca: Mateo said, "Dos (*Pause*), uno, uno, uno (*Pause*), uno" (Figure 5.18). Then "Tres (*Pause*), dos, dos, dos (*Pause*), dos. (*Ms. Ramos records the words.*) Cuatro (*Pause*), tres, tres, tres (*Pause*), tres."

Ms. Ramos: Blanca, you almost sounded like you were singing. "Dos, uno, uno, uno (*Pause*) uno. Tres, dos, dos, dos (*Pause*) dos. Cuatro, tres, tres, tres (*Pause*) tres." (*Pointing to the Spanish*) Who saw this repetition in Mateo's building? What was he doing every time?

Dos . . . uno, uno, uno . . . uno

Tres . . . dos, dos, dos . . . dos

Cuatro . . . tres, tres, tres . . . tres

Figure 5.18

Alexa: Every time he did the same thing. First he took the top off, then he pointed to the row under it, then the front arm, then the right arm, the back arm, and then he put the top back on. So it was like (*Gesturing as he talks*) take the top off, row, front, side, back, put the top back on. Every time.

Ms. Ramos: Alexa, can you describe Mateo's building process one more time as I try to draw it here under Mateo's counting pattern?

Alexa: Take the top off, then left row, front, right side, back row, and top.

Ms. Ramos draws the steps of Mateo's constructing process (Figure 5.19), then repeats Alexa's verbal description, recording the words *left, front, right, back,* and *top* as she speaks.

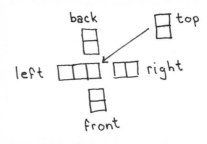

Figure 5.19 ⦿

PART 3: GENERALIZE REPETITION

In Part 3, students are focusing on how to generalize an example of repetition in their thinking. They are given a handout with the pattern reproduced and a lot of white space so that they can annotate the figures and record their steps as they work. Beyond providing another modality in which to work, the act of annotating/recording often results in shortcutting the building process, and helps students see a connection between the steps in their process and a known aspect of the pattern, like the figure number. Note, the bulk of the generalizing takes place in the partner work.

Individual Think Time and Pairs

Projecting instructions, Ms. Ramos prompts students to use the repetition they noticed in one of the building processes to find the number of cubes in Tower 10 without actually building Tower 10 and counting every cube. Students have several minutes of individual think time to work on this task.

Ms. Ramos then transitions the students to partner work where they share how they approached finding the number of cubes in Tower 10 and then together find a

⦿ Using annotation: Ms. Ramos records the repetition in Mateo's counting, then adds a visual and records key descriptive terms—*left, front, right, back,* and *top*—to help all students see the steps of the process and help Mateo access the English description.

rule for determining the number of cubes given in any tower number. She encourages them to ask themselves, *How can I use the repetition to make my rule?* and draws their attention back to where she recorded and annotated repetitions they shared earlier. Finally, she gives each pair a handout with Towers 1–3 reproduced on it that they can use to communicate and track the process they are generalizing.

Alexa and Laurie are working together to write a rule for Tower *N* by generalizing the repetition in their building.

Laurie: How did you find the blocks in Tower 10?

Alexa: I didn't get the number but I would do it the same way with my repetition.

Laurie (*Pushing the handout in front of Alexa*): Show me.

Alexa: Here's what I was thinking. (*Drawing as she talks*) [See Figure 5.20.] Tower 1 is just one. Tower 2 is the cross (*Referring to five cubes that form a plus sign*) and one on top. Tower 3 is the cross, one on each side and two on top. So the next one would be (*Drawing a diagram representing the fourth tower*) the cross, two, two, two, two, and three on top. And then this (*Drawing a diagram representing the fifth tower*) and then it would just keep going. (*Draws diagram for sixth tower.*)

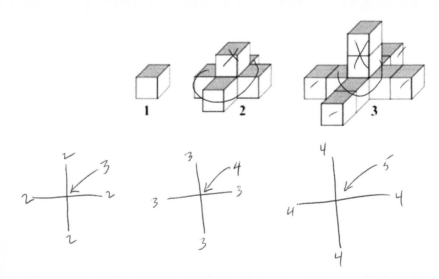

Figure 5.20

Laurie: How many towers do you have there?

Alexa: 1, 2, 3, 4, 5, 6.

Laurie (*Labels the diagrams*): OK, so Tower 4, Tower 5, and Tower 6.

Alexa: It would just keep going that way.

Laurie: So, like this (*Laurie draws Towers 7–10*). [See Figure 5.21.]

Alexa: Yeah.

Laurie (*Referring to Tower 10*): 4 times 8 is 32 plus 9 is 41. So 41 cubes in Tower 10.

Alexa: Yeah. No! You missed some.

Laurie: No, I got the four 8s and the 9.

Alexa: Yeah, but you missed the cross. (*Drawing in the cubes on the cross*) The cross is five blocks. So it's five more . . . 46. [See Figure 5.22.]

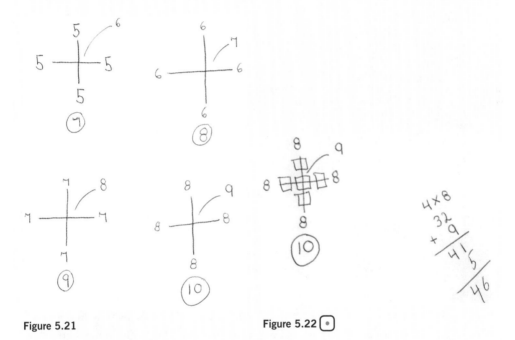

Figure 5.21   **Figure 5.22** 🔘

Laurie: OK. That's for Tower 10. But what's the rule? We have to use your steps to get a rule. 🔘

Alexa: Hmm (*Looking at Tower 10*). It's just five in the cross on the bottom, plus the four arms, plus the middle stack. (*Laurie writes "5 + 4 arms + middle stack" on their paper.*) It's just we don't know how many are in the arms.

🔘 Note that the repetition in Alexa's building process can be seen in the way she records the process. This process residue allows Laurie to adopt Alexa's building process and work with her to generalize the repetition at the center of her process.

🔘 It's common to give some students who struggle a handout with figures reproduced and a table to complete. However, providing a table to complete focuses students' attention on the results and can mask their process. Therefore, Ms. Ramos intentionally gives her students a handout with a lot of white space to record their building process. This recording often results in students consolidating their process as Alexa did.

Laurie: Look, the middle stack is always one more than the arms!

Alexa: Yeah, but what's the arms?

Laurie: The arms keep going up by 1.

Alexa: But that won't help us get big towers because we won't know the one before. We have to (*Pause*) we have to connect the arms to something we do know.

Laurie: Like the tower number.

Alexa: Yeah, like the tower number. Wait! Yeah. Right. The tower number. Look! (*Pointing to Towers 7–9*) 7, 5 (*Pause*) 8, 6 (*Pause*) 9, 7. The tower number is always two more than the arm.

Laurie: So for like 100. Tower 100. It would be 100 minus 2. It would be 98. So 5 plus 98, 98, 98, 98, and 99.

Alexa: Yeah, but how do we write that for *N*?

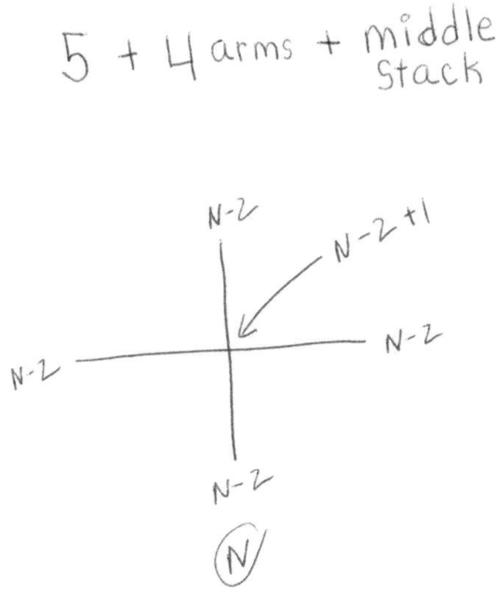

Figure 5.23

(*Alexa draws "Tower* **N**," *labeling each arm* **N** *– 2 and the middle stack* **N** *– 2 + 1. [See Figure 5.23]*)

Laurie: Yes! You got it! The rule is $5 + 4(N - 2) + N - 2 + 1$. I mean $N - 1$. The rule is $5 + 4(N - 2) + N - 1$. ⦿

PARTS 4 AND 5: DISCUSS GENERALIZATIONS AND REFLECT

In Part 4 of the routine, students share generalizations and connect them to the corresponding repeating processes. This helps students gain insights about how mathematical notation can be used to describe a generalized process. This is also a place to press for precision in descriptions and use of academic language. In this part of the routine, the flow from individual think time to pairs to full group sharing collapses into several repeated think-pair-share cycles every time the class considers a new generalization.

> ⦿ Students who struggle to generalize need opportunities to experience and represent repetition in multiple ways before being asked to generalize the repetition. First having the opportunity to build towers helped Alexa notice repetition. Having the handout on which she could then visually represent her building process supported Alexa's move toward generalizing. Explaining the repeating process to her partner and recording it multiple times helped Alexa "own" the repetition. Now with a solid understanding of the pattern, Alexa could focus on connecting the changing "arm values" of her visual representation to a number that she knew (the tower number). Being able to move back and forth between the actual towers, the drawings, the words, and the specific tower numbers helped Alexa be able to represent the rule with algebraic notation.

There were several different rules in the room. Ms. Ramos decided to have the class start with $N + 4(N - 1)$ because it was the most common rule, so more students could easily discuss it. It also contained two clearly recognizable chunks that could be easily connected back to the repetition in the building process.

Ms. Ramos: I am going to put Karen and Larena's work under the document camera. [See Figure 5.24.] Take ten seconds individually to look at their work, and ask yourself, "What is the repetition they are generalizing?"

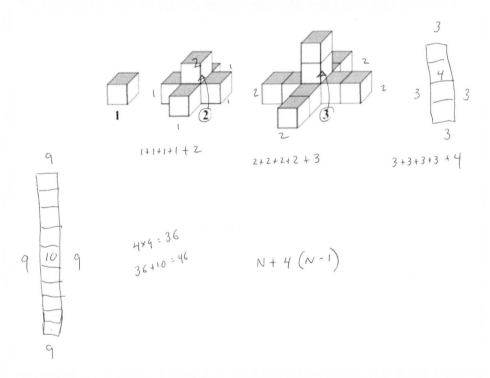

Figure 5.24

Ms. Ramos (*After ten seconds*): OK, turn and talk to your partner. What repetition did they generalize?

Ms. Ramos (*After students talk for a few moments*): What repetition did Larena and Karen generalize? Miguel?

Miguel: $1 + 1 + 1 + 1 + 2, 2 + 2 + 2 + 2 + 3, 3 + 3 + 3 + 3 + 4$. There's four numbers and one more.

Ms. Ramos (*Pointing to the numbers Miguel just read*): Where are these numbers coming from?

Miguel: The sides and the middle of the towers. Every side is the same and the middle is one more. (*Ms. Ramos points to the corresponding pieces of the tower as Miguel speaks.*)

Ms. Ramos: Larena, how did you and Karen turn that repetition into your rule $N + 4$ times the quantity (*Gesturing parenthesis*) $N - 1$?

Larena: The middle is the same as the tower and the sides are 1 less. N for the tower and $N - 1$ for the sides.

Karen: And there are four sides so $4 \times N - 1$.

As Larena and Karen explain, Ms. Ramos annotates. [See Figure 5.25.]

Ms. Ramos: Brianna, would you please restate how Karen and Larena generalized the repetition in their building process? What did they do every time? How did they turn their process into a rule?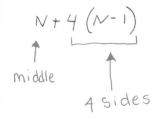

Brianna: Every time they built a tower, they did the middle and then added the four sides. The number of cubes in the middle was always the same as the tower number. And the cubes on the sides were always one less. So they just put it together like they were building—tower number, plus one less, and do that four times. We built the same but our rule is different. We got $N + N - 1 + N - 1 + N - 1 + N - 1$.

(*Ms. Ramos writes $N + N - 1 + N - 1 + N - 1 + N - 1$.*)

Figure 5.25

> ⦿ Ms. Ramos is trying to help students learn how to generalize repetition, so she goes back to the regularity in the building process and how that process was represented and finally generalized. After giving students think time, she specifically prompts them to ask themselves what the repetition is that they are generalizing. Students then have an opportunity to share the repetition they are seeing with their partner before sharing with the full group.

After the class discusses two more generalizations, Ms. Ramos moves the class to reflecting on their thinking. (See Chapter 7 for sample prompts.)

Important Takeaways

Within the vignette you've just read, there are several important points we'd like to underscore about developing repeated reasoning through the routine. Think about how these relate to your own instruction as you use this routine:

- "Look for and express regularity in repeated reasoning" is often talked about as the math practice where "you look for patterns," but the power in looking for patterns lies in seeing patterns in the *process*, as well as in the *results*. So it's important to make that process as visible as possible; don't let students skip the act of building or drawing to recreate the pattern.

- Encourage students to use a variety of senses to identify the repetition, and model that for them. Look for opportunities to not only see a pattern, but also to hear it and feel it.

- A key role for you in this routine is to help students move from their individual ways of seeing the repetition to a generalization. Build from students' own ways of describing the process they see repeating, and use the Four Rs to gradually develop more generalized language for what's happening, before introducing notation.

- If MP7 and MP8 feel similar, they are, in that they both help students move toward generalization. They differ in what students are paying attention to in order to generalize. With a structural avenue of thinking, students pay attention to the chunks or underlying structure of the mathematics; with a repeated reasoning avenue of thinking, students pay attention to regularities in a counting, calculation, or construction process.

- You can use this avenue of thinking in a problem that doesn't have a visual pattern by creating your own repetition. You can substitute values and play out the calculation, not to "guess and check" the correct answer, but to identify the repeated steps that you're doing. Recall in Chapter 1 when Roberto approached the problem of running laps by testing different numbers, not to guess and check the answer, but to look for repetition in his process, so he could generalize the steps.

We've now talked about all three avenues of thinking and how to use them to help students enter a problem and sustain their thinking. However, to make use of them, students need to first make sense of a problem, and these avenues of thinking will inform that problem interpretation. So in the next chapter, we'll return to the first math practice, "Make sense of problems and persevere in solving them," and look at a routine that helps students initially make sense of a problem, and launch into one of these avenues of thinking.

Three Reads

An Instructional Routine to Support Students Entering and Sustaining Thinking in a Problem

Having gotten the attention of his fifth-grade students, Mr. Estefan asked Alexeya to read the problem of the day. Alexeya read:

> *A prince picked a basketful of golden apples in the Enchanted Orchard. On his way home, the prince came to a troll who guarded the orchard. The troll stopped him and demanded payment of one-half of the apples plus 2 more, so the prince gave him the apples and set off again. A little further on, he encountered a second troll. The second troll demanded payment of one-half of the apples the prince now had plus 2 more. The prince paid him, and set off once more. Just before leaving the Enchanted Orchard, a third troll stopped him and demanded one-half of his remaining apples plus 2 more. The prince paid him and sadly went home. He had only 2 golden apples left. How many apples had he picked?*

Mr. Estefan thanked Alexeya for reading the problem, turned to the class, and asked, "So, what is this problem asking you to do?" Waiting a few seconds, he called on Pedro. "Pedro, tell us what the problem is asking."

Pedro replied, "Find out how many apples he had picked."

"Great. So your job is to answer the question, 'How many apples had he picked?' Any questions?" Again, Mr. Estefan waited a few seconds. No one had a question so he said, "Go ahead and get started on the Trolls problem. You can work on your own or with your tablemate. I'll be around to answer any questions."

He quickly checked attendance then began touring the room. When he walked up to the first table, Lily looked up at him and said, "I don't get it."

When a student says, "I don't get it," many teachers we know respond with "What don't you get?" If the student can't tell them, they proceed to explain the problem over again, laying out the steps to solve it. The teacher might say:

The prince picked some apples. We don't know how many he picked. But we do have clues that we can use to determine how many apples the prince picked initially. We know he ended with 2 apples. So we can work backward. What's the last thing the prince did before he came out of the orchard with his measly 2 apples?

They then backtrack the student through the transaction with the third troll, adding 2 and then multiplying by 2.

So 2 + 2 is 4 and 4 × 2 is 8. That means the prince had eight apples when he met the third troll.

In some cases, they then encourage students to use the same line of thinking with the second and first trolls; in other cases, they continue and complete the problem with the student. If they have an opportunity to move on to other students, they find themselves having the same conversation. With the best of intentions to support students in their work, these teachers are actually doing all the thinking for the students, leaving the students dependent on the teacher in any future problem-solving situations. But what other choice do they have? The answer lies in rethinking the interactions and questions that teachers pose to students when first making sense of a problem. Rather than focusing on helping each student "get the answer," you can help your students *make sense of the problem*.

Entering a Problem and Sustaining the Thinking: Two Key Ideas of Math Practice 1

In the first chapter, we described math practice (MP) 1, *Make sense of problems and persevere in solving them*, as the umbrella practice under which the other seven math practices sit. We consider *entering the problem* and *sustaining the thinking* to be the two key ideas of MP1.

Entering a Problem: Building Students' Capacity to "Get It"

By *entering a problem*, we mean that first students need to be able to read and interpret the problem, to understand the problem context and the question or questions they are being asked, and to identify the important problem information. Recall the vignette at the start of this chapter where Mr. Estefan's students set off to work on the problem of the day. The class could read the task and identify the question to be answered: How many apples had he picked? However, it was clear from the "I-don't-get-its" that simply reading the words and plucking the question off the page was not sufficient. The students needed to see that it was not just a story about a prince and trolls in an enchanted orchard, but a problem about some number of apples that was decreased by "a half and 2 more" three different times, leaving only two apples remaining in the end. The students needed to get past the noise of the context to the mathematically relevant aspects of the problem. They needed to read like a mathematician.

Sustaining the Thinking: Building Students' Capacity to Get Themselves Unstuck

Students can sustain their thinking and persevere through difficult problem-solving experiences if they have at least one accessible way into a problem and alternative avenues to take if the approach they choose does not lead them to a solution method. Here again, we leverage the three avenues of mathematical thinking.

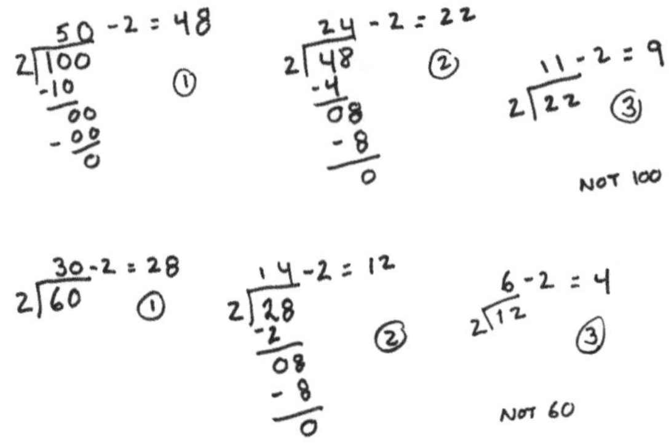

Figure 6.1

For example, let's look at Roberto, who starts by just trying out some numbers (Figure 6.1). He first guesses 100 as the starting number, divides by 2, then subtracts 2, then carries out the rest of the calculations to end up with 9, and concludes the starting number was not 100. He also tests 60, gets a result of 4, and concludes the answer is not 60.

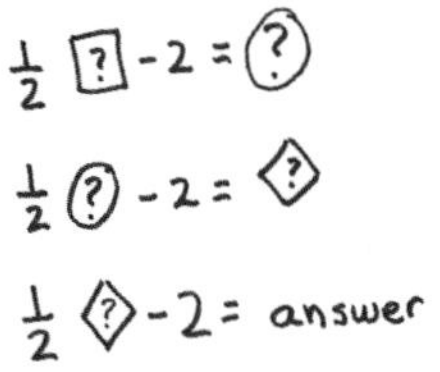

He tries a few more numbers, none of which result in the correct answer of two apples. He notices that each time, he is doing the same thing: divide by 2, then subtract 2, and that he does that three times to try to get two apples. He tries writing an equation (Figure 6.2), but he can't figure out how to use his equation to find an answer.

Figure 6.2

Roberto looks over at the "Think Like a Mathematician" wall where his teacher has posted ask-yourself questions. (See Figure 6.3.)

Ask yourself . . .		
Think Quantities!	**Think Structure!**	**Think Repetition!**
• What can I count? • What can I measure? • How are the quantities related? • How can I represent the quantities so I can see the relationships?	• How is this situation behaving? • What kind of problem is this? • Does this problem remind me of another I've solved? • Will changing the form help? • How can I chunk this expression/number/visual?	• Is there a process that keeps repeating? • Am I counting/building/ drawing in the same way each time? • Do I keep repeating the same set of calculations? • How can I use repetition to write a rule?

Figure 6.3

He scans the list of questions and stops at "What kind of problem is this?" Roberto thinks, *Well, it's one of those problems that has a repeating process, where you know the ending, but you don't know the start. What if I worked the process backward? Could I do that?* Roberto wonders. Having clearly identified the string of calculations in the repeated one-half-plus-2-more process, and knowing that the process results in two apples, Roberto tries thinking his process backward to determine the number of apples at the start. First, Roberto writes down the series of repeating calculations he tried to represent with an algebraic equation and puts a 2 at the end (Figure 6.4). Then he starts working backward from the 2, undoing each of the calculations, until he reaches the starting point, 44 (Figure 6.5).

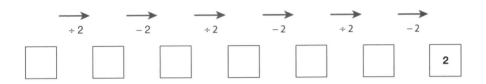

Figure 6.4

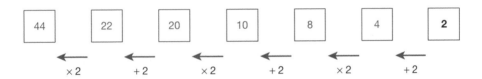

Figure 6.5

The key to sustaining the thinking is having options. A student who can reason abstractly and quantitatively, look for and make use of structure, and look for and express regularity in repeated reasoning has mathematical options for ways of reasoning about a problem. If one line of reasoning is not working, a student can engage another. In this way, students can persevere through particularly challenging math problems. Over time, this perseverance develops a healthy problem-solving disposition.

Reading Mathematics Is Not Like Reading Other Text

Reading in math—especially reading a math word problem—is different from reading in other subject areas. One reason is that the purpose for reading—identifying and answering some mathematical question—doesn't come until the end of the word problem. Instead of starting with a topic sentence or main idea, a math problem starts by presenting a litany of details (e.g., a prince picked apples in an enchanted orchard, he met a troll and had to give that troll one half of the apples he picked plus 2 more, he then met a second troll, and so on). It is only when you get to the end of the word problem, to the question that is being asked, that you know why you are reading—in our example, this is to find out how many apples the prince picked.

Another reason is that word problems are often a combination of both narrative and expository text; narrative text tells a story and expository text provides information. In a typical word problem, expository text gives information about relationships, comparisons, causes and effects, and sequencing but often does so within narrative text, a story, or real-world context. So when reading a word problem, you have to read for the math "hidden" underneath the context. It's the difference between saying "The problem is about trolls and apples" and saying "The problem is about some number of apples that was decreased by a half and 2 more three different times, leaving only two apples remaining in the end."

Therefore, word problems must be read several times, with a different focus each time so that the reader can understand the situation, identify the question to be answered, and decide what mathematically important information given in the problem statement will be useful in solving the problem. We advocate teaching students to read a word problem three times with the following focus each time:

1. Read for context. Read the problem quickly to get a general understanding. Ask yourself: *What's the problem about?*

2. Read for question. Read the problem a second time to identify and interpret the question(s) you are asked to answer. Ask yourself: *What am I trying to find out?*

3. Read for information. Now that you know what the problem is about and the question you are trying to answer, read the problem a third time to identify mathematically important information given that you need to solve the problem. Ask yourself: *What is the important information in this problem?*

In many ways, the focus of each of these readings of a math problem parallels what students have learned in their English language arts classes about reading for context, identifying the author's purpose, and determining importance. The *Three Reads* instructional routine formalizes this process for reading and interpreting a math problem.

An Overview of the Three Reads Routine

The Three Reads routine is a slightly different animal from the instructional routines in the previous chapters. In those chapters, we focused much of the discussion on how the routine supported students' use of different mathematical reasoning skills. Our discussion here, however, will be a little different, because Three Reads is designed to support students entering any one of those avenues of thinking. This chapter will make far more sense if you are familiar with at least one of the avenues of thinking and its corresponding routine, so we recommend you read at least one of Chapters 3 through 5 first.

The Steps of the Routine

The Three Reads routine has four parts. Unlike the other routines in this book, it does not end with a student reflection. The four parts of the routine include the launch (Part 1) and then Parts 2–4 that correspond to the three different purposes for reading. But this routine makes use of the same core elements and essential strategies as the other routines.

These next sections provide a brief overview of the four parts of the routine. Later, we provide a classroom illustration of what this routine looks like in action, and we highlight particular supports for special populations.

Part 1: *Launch the Routine*

When launching the routine, the teacher identifies the goal for the routine and reviews its steps. It is important that students understand that they will be looking for different information during each read of the problem, and that this is not yet a time to be doing any calculating or problem solving.

Steps for Part 1

Introduce the Routine

1. Articulate the purpose and flow of the routine to students.

Part 2: *First Read—Understanding the Context*

This first read of the problem takes only a few minutes and is intended to help students focus in a very general sense on what the problem is about. This is not a place to delve into great detail about what the problem is asking.

Steps for Part 2

Individual Think Time

1. Students read the problem and ask themselves, *What's this problem about?* Although we say, "Students read the problem," you may want to choose to read it aloud to the whole class, have a student read it aloud, or use another support strategy to help those students who may struggle with reading the problem. Give them a moment to think about the question, "What's this problem about?"

Part 3: *Second Read—Interpreting the Question*

Students now read the problem a second time, this time with an eye toward determining the question or questions to be answered in the problem. The think-pair-share structure of the second read provides students the opportunity to restate and rephrase the question several times.

Steps for Part 3

Individual Think Time

1. Students read the problem and ask themselves, *What am I trying to find out?* This is an opportunity for students to identify what the goal of the problem is.

Pairs

2. Students work together to articulate the question in their own words. This does not need very much time. However, it's an important step that allows students to rephrase the purpose of the problem.

Full Group Share

3. (Share) Call on a pair of students to offer a possible wording of the problem question.

4. (Rephrase/Reword) Ask one or more students to rephrase the first wording of the question.

5. (Record) Record one or two different framings of the question to be answered.

Part 4: *Third Read—Identifying Important Information*

Students read the problem a third and final time, reading for information given in the problem statement that will be critical to solving the problem. Here, students can draw on (and the teacher should explicitly prompt them to draw on) what they have learned to attend to and ask themselves when reasoning quantitatively, thinking structurally, and reasoning with repetition.

We deliberately hold off the search for important information until after students have a sense of the context (first read) and know what question they are supposed to answer (second read). It is only at this point that students are in a position to identify information given in the problem statement that will be useful in solving the problem, using their own wording of the context and question.

Steps for Part 4

Pairs

1. In the final read, students talk with a partner to identify important information. Depending on what they notice and pay attention to, they may lean toward one of the three avenues of thinking:

   - What are the important quantities and relationships in this problem?

   - How is this situation behaving?

   - Is there a process that keeps repeating that I can generalize?

Full Group Share

2. Students share, rephrase and reword important information. The teacher records their thoughts about what information is important and helps students connect what they noticed and focused on to one of the avenues of thinking.

Note that there is no reflection specified in this routine, as there is in other routines. The entire routine-at-a-glance is shown in Figure 6.6. As you look at the routines across these chapters, note the parallels between the flow of each routine; this can help you become familiar with them more easily.

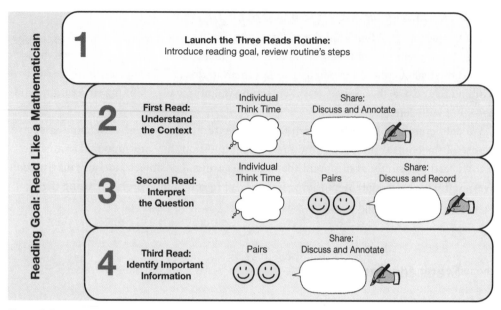

Figure 6.6

Essential Strategies in the Routine

Although all the essential strategies are involved in this routine, the essential strategies of ask-yourself questions and the Four Rs are particularly crucial for providing focus and access in this routine.

Essential Strategies

- Ask-yourself questions
- Annotation
- Sentence frames and sentence starters
- Four Rs: repeat, rephrase, reword, record

Ask-Yourself Questions

Ask-yourself questions focus students on the purpose of each read. In addition, ask-yourself questions are used in Part 4 as a way to help students choose one of the avenues of thinking to start with as they enter the problem.

These questions provide focus and scaffolding for struggling readers who must first work to understand the narrative layer of the word problem before they can comprehend the mathematics underneath the story. Similarly, starting with the "What's this problem about?" ask-yourself question (and subsequent discussion) provides an initial focus on context, which is a crucial first step for English learners, who are more likely to be unfamiliar with the context or language, to enter the problem.

Questions that are especially relevant to this routine include:

- What's this problem about?
- What am I trying to find out?
- What is the important information in this problem?
- What are the important quantities and relationships? (MP2 avenue of thinking)
- How is this situation behaving? (MP7 avenue of thinking)
- Is there a process that keeps repeating? (MP8 avenue of thinking)

Four Rs: *Repeat, Rephrase, Reword, Record*

The use of Four Rs during whole-class discussion helps students build a deeper understanding of the language in the problem. The discussion in the second read functions as an opportunity to repeat, rephrase, and record the goal of the problem, providing additional processing time for those students who need it, and ensuring that everyone begins the problem understanding the goal. In the discussion in the third read, the teacher prompts students to rephrase and reword to help make connections between the students' different areas of focus and the corresponding avenues of thinking.

Challenges, Opportunities, and Supports for Students with Specific Needs

The structure of the Three Reads routine is especially designed to support both students with certain learning disabilities and English language learners (ELLs).

Students with Learning Disabilities

For students to persevere in solving problems, they must first be able to make sense of the problem situation. When language and reading challenges interfere with students' capacity to read and interpret math problems, students often shut down and feel defeated at the outset. The Three Reads instructional routine is designed intentionally to provide access to the mathematics and also to help students develop their capacity to read and interpret math problems.

The Trolls word problem, at the beginning of this chapter, is typical of math word problems as it contains long dense sentences with multiple clauses that need to be unpacked. Students may struggle with understanding the language or meaning of sentences, discerning relevant information, remembering details from the beginning of the problem, or keeping track of steps as they make sense of the rest of the problem. The

Three Reads instructional routine provides students with multiple passes at text interpretation as they are asked at different points to listen, read along, read aloud, picture and discuss the text individually, with a partner, and in the full group, supporting those students with working memory and other reading-related struggles. These multiple passes provide students with multiple opportunities to hear, read, and comprehend the language in the word problem.

During the routine, each read centers around a particular question that focuses student reading to either make sense of the context ("What's this problem about?"), locate the main idea ("What is the question to be answered?"), or determine the importance of the information given in the text ("What important information is given?"). All three of these questions focus on critical components of reading comprehension and language development. Locating the main idea, in particular, is heralded as a high-leverage reading strategy. After multiple experiences with the Three Reads routine, students internalize a process that they can apply as they approach future complex problem situations.

Supporting Students with Learning Disabilities When Using This Routine

- Provide students multiple passes at interpreting the problem.
- Emphasize ask-yourself questions to develop students' internal dialogue.
- Record (and/or have students record) students' responses throughout the Three Reads routine to support multiple modalities.

English Language Learners

Reading and interpreting math word problems is challenging for all students, but it is especially difficult for ELLs. ELLs need to make sense of an unfamiliar context and unfamiliar vocabulary while trying to build new mathematical understanding. The routine supports students' access to the mathematics and builds independence by unpacking problem contexts without removing students' opportunities to reason mathematically about the problem.

Providing access to the context can be as simple as adding some pictures and icons to illustrate a story context. Alternatively, students can act out the scenario along with the first read. Rephrasing helps students make sense of the context, as it prompts sense making, helps connect new words to known words, and allows students to hear self-talk. The strategy you choose to ensure that students can understand the problem context needs to position English learners so that they can respond to the first-read question, "What's this problem about?" Subsequent reads and discussion will unpack more of the language.

The discussion of the text on the second and third read provides ELLs with multiple opportunities to both hear and read the language in the word problem. Reading aloud to a partner provides English learners a less stressful environment in which to practice producing the language.

Problems like the Trolls problem contain any number of words and phrases that an English learner may not yet know. The key is to identify those words or phrases that are critical to the mathematical interpretation of the problem statement, and focus on those words. If special populations are going to have access to the same learning opportunity as their classmates, they need to know the meaning of the phrase "now had" (i.e., the second troll demanded payment of one-half the apples the prince *now had* plus two more) and the meaning of the word *remaining* (i.e., a third troll stopped him and demanded one-half of his *remaining* apples plus two more), as these are critical to determining the number of apples that the prince has.

In addition, an ELL may not know what the words *enchanted* or *basketful* mean. Those words are not critical to unpacking the mathematics behind the context, so why include them, potentially adding a layer of language complexity? We point back to our guiding principle of putting students in a language-rich environment and our belief that it's important to take every opportunity to help ELLs develop language. Supporting ELLs involves a balancing act between two opposing realities. On the one hand, life doesn't simplify language for ELLs, and they need to encounter as much language as they can while in a supportive environment that can help them learn to make sense of it. On the other hand, every teacher wants to be sensitive to the cognitive and language loads on students and not overwhelm them unnecessarily. Every teacher needs to make his or her own decision about what language loads are appropriate for his or her students.

Supporting English Language Learners When Using This Routine

- Develop enough understanding of the context so that it is not a barrier for ELLs to participate, particularly in the first read.

- Consider the essential words and phrases that are critical for a comprehensive understanding of the mathematics that underlies the context.

- Provide students multiple opportunities to produce language as they make sense of a problem.

Three Reads in Action

The following vignette provides an illustration of the Three Reads routine, focusing on ways it supports students with learning disabilities and ELLs.

In this vignette, we're looking in on Mr. Estefan's fifth-grade class, which has been working on solving problems involving multiplication and division of fractions. The students in this class have fairly solid math skills, but they have struggled with reading and interpreting word problems on their own. The class has worked with the Three Reads instructional routine four times already, so the students (and the teacher!) are now familiar with its flow. (For more information on how to first introduce the routine to students, see Chapter 7.)

Classroom Snapshot: Mr. Estefan's Fifth-Grade Math Class

There is a wide range of learners in Mr. Estefan's fifth-grade math class. Some students you will meet include:

- Tia and Lily, who each have an Individualized Education Program (IEP):
  - Tia struggles with conceptual processing. She is a concrete learner. She has strong social skills and does well when working with a partner or in a small group. Supports identified in her IEP include use of models, manipulatives, and movement breaks during class.
  - Lily has weak visual-spatial processing, but is a strong verbal processor. She participates fully in class discussion, though her written work is disorganized and often incomplete.
- The ELLs include Mariana, Luiz, Julia, and Pedro. They are all of Brazilian origin and speak Portuguese.
  - Mariana has most recently been assessed at an English language development proficiency level 4.
  - Luis was assessed at an English language development proficiency level 2 but formal observation suggests he may be closer to a level 3.
  - Pedro and Julia have both tested out of an ELL designation, but Mr. Estefan continues to provide language support, especially writing support. Their Portuguese is strong and so Mr. Estefan often depends on them to translate for other ELLs in the classroom.

PARTS 1 AND 2: LAUNCH AND FIRST READ—UNDERSTANDING THE CONTEXT

The purpose of this first part of the Three Reads routine is to orient students to the math problem. The teacher explains the purpose of the routine—to learn how to read and interpret a math problem—and describes the steps or flow of the routine. The teacher reads the problem for the first time and gives students some silent processing time, then several students share with the class what they think the problem is about.

Introduce the Routine

Mr. Estefan: Yesterday we started looking at strategies for problem solving. We're going to look at a new problem today. As usual, we will read the problem three times as we make sense of it. (*Mr. Estefan points to where he has posted the Three Reads questions on the wall.*) First, read and think: *What is this problem about?* Second, read and think: *What is the question?* Third, read and think: *What information is important?* The problem has a longer story to it than some others we've worked on, so today I am going to ask a few of you to act out the scenario when we do our first read. I need four volunteers, someone to read and three people to act out being trolls. (•)

(•) Note that Mr. Estefan no longer includes a formal launch for the Three Reads. This is the fifth time he has used the routine and the students have internalized the purpose and flow.

Individual Think Time

Mr. Estefan selects Alexeya to read because he knows she can read loudly and clearly articulate each word. He chooses three other students to play the trolls, including Tia who benefits from movement during class. He asks each troll to stand along the front board underneath where he has written *Troll #1*, *Troll #2*, and *Troll #3*. Mr. Estefan places a paper crown on his own head, picks up a basket with yellow cubes in it to represent golden apples, and assumes the role of the prince. Mr. Estefan reminds Alexeya to read slowly, pausing at the end of each sentence for the action to take place. As Alexeya reads, Mr. Estefan acts out giving each troll one-half of his apples and then two more. At the end, Mr. Estefan displays an exaggerated frown and shows a basket with just two apples. The class applauds. (•)

> **Mr. Estefan** (*Bowing*): So, what's this problem about? (*He waits, giving students a few seconds to think.*)

Full-Group Share

Mr. Estefan calls on various students to share their understanding of the context with the full group. At one point, he stops and presses one student who describes the trolls as "greedy" to explain what she means. Mr. Estefan quickly records the ideas on the whiteboard in two columns underneath the title "This problem is about...." (Figure 6.7) (••) :

Context	Math
A prince	Taking half
Apples	Finding out how many apples the prince picked
A prince picking apples	Subtraction
Paying with apples	Writing an equation
Greedy trolls	Working backward
A lot of effort for just 2 apples	

Figure 6.7

(•) Mr. Estefan opted to act out the scenario during the first read because the problem statement was full of unfamiliar language that could create a stumbling block for his ELLs. By acting out the story, the ELLs could quickly understand the situation, at least enough to answer the first question, "What's this problem about?" Students do not yet need to read the text themselves; an articulate English-speaking student is modeling language production. Students now have some private think time to process the language and develop a mental image.

(••) Keeping the first question—"What's this problem about?"—intentionally open-ended invites all students into the sense making. Separating out student contributions into two columns, "Context" and "Math," helps students start to distinguish between the two, as they will eventually learn to focus primarily on the mathematical responses.

Students now identify and clarify the question that the problem is asking. The think-pair-share structure, combined with rephrasing the question, gives students multiple opportunities to clarify their understanding and allows time for ELLs and any students who struggle with language to process and practice verbalizing the wording of the question before sharing in the full group.

Individual Think Time and Pairs

Mr. Estefan (*Holding up two fingers and pointing again to the Three Reads poster*): OK, second read. Now that we know a little something about the context, let's read the problem a second time to identify the question we're supposed to answer. The second read is a think-pair-share. (*He points to the Think-Pair-Share poster on the wall that reviews the steps of think-pair-share that students have used frequently.*) ⦿

Mr. Estefan asks Pedro to read, and reminds him to read slowly and loudly enough that everyone can hear. He projects the problem so that students can read along. He reminds students they are listening and thinking *What's the question we're asked to answer?* After Pedro reads, Mr. Estefan says:

Mr. Estefan: Take fifteen seconds of individual think time (*Mr. Estefan points to his head as he says* think). So in this problem about "paying with apples" (*He points to some of the responses on the class chart*) and "greedy trolls," and "taking half," what is the question? What are you trying to find out? Think about how you would state the question in your own words. OK, together with your partner, come up with a clear—precise—wording of the question. You have one minute. (*Mr. Estefan quickly tours the room listening in on partner conversations.*)

Full-Group Share

Mr. Estefan: So, in your own words, what's the question we need to answer? Arushi and Aviva, how did you reword the question?

Aviva: We're supposed to figure out how many apples the prince had.

Arushi: To start, how many apples the prince had at the start, before he met the trolls trying to get out of the enchanted orchard.

Mr. Estefan: Who would like to rephrase what Aviva and Arushi offered, putting it in the form of a question?

Lily: How many apples did the prince have at the start before he gave any to the trolls?

Mr. Estefan (*Recording the question on the front board*): Raise your hand if you worded the question similarly. (*All hands in the room go up except Mariana and Julia.*) Mariana, how did you and Julia phrase the question?

(*Mariana and Julia speak softly to each other, then Mariana says*): What was the number of apples . . ."

⦿ Mr. Estefan is using gestures here to provide additional support for students to understand what he is saying. Look for ways that he does this throughout the routine.

Julia: . . . the prince picked?

Mariana: . . . the prince picked?

Mr. Estefan: What was the number of apples the prince picked? Mariana, can you say the whole question again please?

Mariana: What was the number of apples the prince picked?

Mr. Estefan: Great. Who can rephrase Mariana and Julia's wording of the question? Pedro? ⦿

Pedro: Me and Luiz said, "What was the total number of apples picked?" (*Mr. Estefan records this new wording of the question on the board beneath the question Lily framed.*)

Mr. Estefan (*Pointing to both recorded questions*): Are these two questions asking the same thing? (*Pausing a few seconds*) What do you think, Tia?

Tia: Yes.

Mr. Estefan: Explain your thinking.

Tia: We said we needed to know how many apples the prince had at the start and that's the apples he picked before he had to give some away to the three trolls.

Mr. Estefan: Oh, so you're saying that in your question *at the start* means the number of apples the prince picked.

Tia: Yeah, the story starts with the prince picking a bunch of apples. Those were the cubes you had in your basket.

(*Mr. Estefan circles* at the start, *draws an arrow pointing to it, and writes "# of apples picked," then moves the class to the third read.*) [See Figure 6.8.]

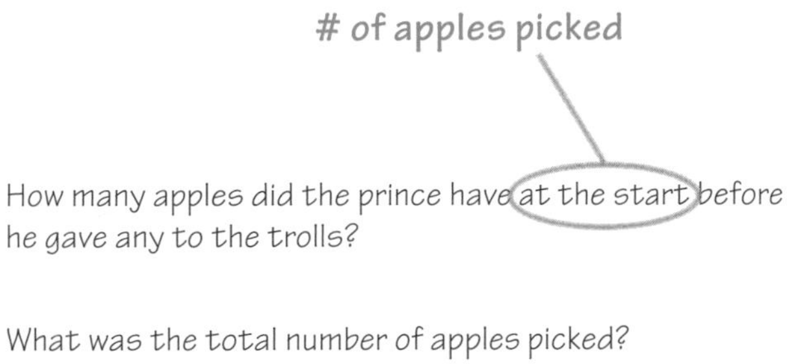

# of apples picked

How many apples did the prince have at the start before he gave any to the trolls?

What was the total number of apples picked?

Figure 6.8 ⦂

⦿ Having the opportunity to talk briefly with Julia provides Mariana a safe place to work out how she will verbalize her mathematical idea in English. Mr. Estefan then models the academic language by repeating Mariana and Julia's question, then asks Mariana to restate the question altogether to provide her with an opportunity to practice the language.

⦂ Once students have had practice identifying the question and stating it in their own words, the teacher can begin to transition students from the "story" part of the context to the mathematics lurking under the surface. We can see this in the vignette as the class' phrasing of the question evolves from "How many apples did the prince have at the start before he gave any to the trolls?" to "What was the total number of apples picked?" Mr. Estefan supports this transition by asking students to connect the "number of apples picked" wording in the second question to the first question. Then he annotates that connection, leaving the annotation visible for students to refer back to. This annotation also supports weak auditory processors and plays to the strength of strong visual processors, while at the same time leaving visual residue of an important mathematical idea for students who struggle with attention issues.

PART 4: THIRD READ—IDENTIFYING IMPORTANT INFORMATION

In this last part of the routine, students read for important information, and depending on what they notice and pay attention to, can begin with one of the avenues of thinking. Partners are asked to take on the role of reader or recorder. This presents an opportunity for English learners to practice language production, either reading the word problem in a low-stress environment to a partner or practicing writing down the important information that the pair identifies (in this example, these students will be readers). Having partners work together to make sense of the word problem, determining the importance of key information and attaching mathematics meaning to the context, continues to support reading comprehension.

Pairs

Mr. Estefan: So we know what our problem is about (*Pointing to the recorded responses to the first read*): We have "greedy trolls" who make the prince "pay with apples." And we know what we are trying to figure out (*Pointing to the recorded questions*): "How many apples did the prince have to start before he gave any to the trolls?" or, said another way, "What was the total number of apples picked?" (*Holding up three fingers*) Third read. So, now we are in a very good position to read the problem a third time to determine mathematically important information—information that will help us find out the "total number of apples picked by the prince." ⦿

Mr. Estefan: With your partner, identify the important information. (*He points to a handout he is holding*) Each pair will get this handout with the problem at the top and room underneath to record important information. (*Pointing to the windows and then to his eyes*) Students on the window side will read. (*Pointing to the door and then gesturing writing*) Students on the door side will record. Raise your hand if you are the reader. (*Mr. Estefan checks to make sure roles are clear.*) Read the problem out loud to your partner. Together, identify important information. The recorder should write the important information down on this handout. Tia, would you please give one copy of this handout to each pair? Lily, would you please repeat the instructions for us?

Lily: One of us reads the problem aloud, then we find important problem information and the recorder writes it down.

Mr. Estefan: Perfect. Go ahead and get started. You have five minutes.

Mr. Estefan has strategically grouped his students so that the English learners are sitting on the "window side" of each table and are partnered with English-speaking students. This allows him to easily differentiate roles as he did here by assigning the ELLs to read the word problem rather than record the information.

> ⦿ By using both versions of the question, Mr. Estefan is supporting a range of learners in the classroom—those for whom sticking closely to the story aspect of the context is helpful and those who may benefit from a less dense—if more abstract—sentence.

Mr. Estefan tours the room, listening and looking for which avenue of thinking students are using: are they attending to quantities and relationships, mathematical structure, or repetition of a process? Following are three samples.

Luiz: Important information?

Pedro: He gives away half the apples and then two more to the first troll.

Luiz: Half and two, second troll.

Pedro: And the third troll.

Luiz: Every time, half and two more. Write that.

Pedro (*Talking as he writes*): The prince gives away half of his apples, plus two more to every troll he meets.

Mr. Estefan notes that Luiz and Pedro, like several other pairs, are attending to the repetition in the process. When he moves over to Lily and Tia, he hears a different conversation. Lily and Tia are not focusing so much on the "half and two more" repeating process as they are focusing on the quantities in the story and how they are related to each other.

Tia: We know there are only two apples at the end.

Lily: So the number of apples at the end is two. Write that down.

Tia (*Writing # of apples at the end is 2 on the paper*): OK. So we know how many apples at the end. How many apples does he give to the first troll?

Lily: We don't know. We know the number of apples he gave the first troll was half of the number of apples he picked, plus two more.

Tia: OK, so the first troll gets half the apples the prince picked, plus two more. And the second troll gets half of what's left, plus two more.

Lily: So, the number of apples the third troll gets is half . . . half of the . . . the number of apples. Um, the number of apples the prince had after he left the second troll, plus two more.

Tia: How should I write that down?

Lily: How about, the number of apples each troll gets is half the number the prince has, plus two more?

Tia: But it's different each time because the prince has already given some of his apples away.

Mr. Estefan considers what he has heard and decides that, during the full group share-out, he will try to highlight the two different avenues of mathematical thinking he is hearing in the room—attention to repetition (MP8) and attention to quantities and relationships (MP2). ⦿

⦿ Mr. Estefan decides to highlight the repetition first because more students started there, and because thinking about the process of giving away half of the apples and two more connects more closely to the storyline of the context; starting here will allow students to review the context and will support students who are still using the story to process their thinking. He will turn to the second approach later, as it requires a bit more interpretation and abstraction.

Full-Group Share

Mr. Estefan: What's a piece of information given in the problem statement that you think might be important or helpful when solving this problem? Pedro and Luiz, why don't you start us off?

Pedro: The prince gave away half of his apples, plus two more to the first troll. And then he gave away half of his apples and two more to the second troll. And he did the same when he met the last troll.

Mr. Estefan: Luiz, how should I record this information for the group?

Luiz (*Reading from their paper*): The prince gives away half of his apples, plus two more to every troll he meets. (*Mr. Estefan writes* Important Information, *underlines it, and then records Luiz' statement underneath it on the board. As he's doing so, he asks students to raise their hand if they too identified this important information. Many hands go up.*)

Mr. Estefan: Ah, so you all are reading like mathematicians. You paid attention to a process that kept repeating. Julia (*whose hand was raised*), what's the process that keeps repeating? What keeps happening? Every time . . . ⊙

Julia: Every time the prince meets a troll, he gives that troll half of his apples, plus two more.

Mr. Estefan: Great. Mathematicians look for and then make use of repetition—something that keeps happening or repeating—in their problem solving. Maybe some of you will make use of this repeating process. Tia and Lily, it seemed like you two were paying attention to something else when you were identifying important information. Why don't you share some of the important information you wrote down. (*To the class*) While Lily and Tia share, think about what they were paying attention to.

Tia: We wrote down *number of apples at the end is 2* and *the number of apples each troll gets is half of the number the prince has plus 2 more*. (*Mr. Estefan quickly records the statements next to the first piece of information.*) [See Figure 6.9.]

Important Information	
• # of apples at the end is 2. • # of apples each troll gets is $\frac{1}{2}$ the # of apples the prince has, plus 2.	• Every time, the prince gives a troll half of his apples plus 2 more.

Figure 6.9

⊙ Mr. Estefan highlights for the class the repeated reasoning avenue of thinking many of them used to interpret the problem. He points out that they were paying attention to a process that keeps repeating. Then he asks Julia, a student who self-identified as noticing the repetition, to articulate the repeating process, providing a familiar sentence starter, "Every time. . . ."

Mr. Estefan: Look at the statement Luiz gave us on the right and the two statements Tia offered on the left. Think. How they are different? (*Mr. Estefan waits ten seconds while the students silently consider.*) OK, quick turn and talk with your partner: How are the statements different? What were Lily and Tia were paying attention to? What were Luiz and Pedro attending to as they looked for important information?

(As the pairs talk, Mr. Estefan writes the following sentence frame on the board.)

Luiz and Pedro paid attention to _____

but Lily and Tia paid attention to _____.

Mr. Estefan (*Bringing the class back together*): Who thinks they can explain what is different about what each pair paid attention to? You can use the sentence frame if it helps. Aviva?

Aviva: Arushi and I were saying that like us, Luiz and Pedro paid attention to how the half and two more kept repeating but Lily and Tia paid attention to how much apples there are.

Mr. Estefan: Can you say some more about what you mean by "how much apples there are"?

Aviva: How much apples there are. Like, at the end there are two and like, how many apples the trolls get.

Mr. Estefan: Lily, Tia, do Aviva and Arushi have it right? Were you paying attention to the number of apples at different points in the story?

Lily: Yeah. We were given the number of apples at the end. But we didn't know how many apples the prince picked or how many apples each troll got.

Tia: I was kind of picturing the cubes in the basket, and how many cubes you were taking out of the basket and giving to each of us.

Mr. Estefan: So Lily and Tia were reading like mathematicians too, only instead of reading for repetition, they were reading for quantities, things they could count, like the number of apples in a basket. (*Mr. Estefan points to the MP2, MP7, and MP8 avenues of thinking ask-yourself questions that are posted on the wall.*) When mathematicians read for important information in a word problem, they often read for quantities—the things that can be counted or measured in the problem. Sometimes we are given the value of those quantities—like the number of apples the prince had at the end is two—and sometimes we're not given a value—like the number of apples each troll gets or the number of apples the prince picked. So, what kind of information do mathematicians think is important to read for in a word problem? Lily?

Lily: Quantities.

Mr. Estefan: And what's a quantity?

Lily: Something you can count, like the number of apples.

Mr. Estefan: What other kind of information do mathematicians think is important?

Arushi: Things that keep happening.

Mr. Estefan: Things that keep happening or repeating.

(*Mr. Estefan fills in the sentence stem blanks with* repetition *and* quantities.)

    Luiz and Pedro paid attention to <u>REPETITION,</u>

    but Lily and Tia paid attention to <u>QUANTITIES</u>.

So when mathematicians read for important information, they can be reading for a process that keeps repeating, or they can be reading for quantities. There are other things mathematicians pay attention to when they are reading and interpreting a word problem that we'll talk about another day. But for now, see if you can think like a mathematician and make use of either the repetition or what you know about the quantities in this word problem to determine how many apples the prince picked. ⊙

> ⊙ Not every task will invite all three avenues of mathematical thinking. And you don't have to talk about every avenue you see when students identify important information. In the vignette, Mr. Estefan did not hear evidence of students reasoning structurally. That could be because they have not yet developed that avenue of thinking, or it could be that the task didn't invite structural thinking, or he simply missed it. Regardless, his students are now at a mathematical crossroads: they can choose which avenue of thinking to follow through the problem. And they know there is not just one route.

Deciding When and How to Have Students Reflect

Note there is no formal "Math Practice Reflection" step built into the Three Reads routine to bring it to a close. The reason is that typically after Part 4 of the Three Reads, students begin to solve the problem. Our own experience using this routine shows us that stopping at this point to ask students to reflect on what they have learned about reading and interpreting a math problem interrupts a natural momentum that students start to feel about digging in and starting to work on the problem.

However, asking students to reflect on what they are learning about making sense of a math problem is important and doesn't necessarily need to be done right at the end of the routine. You might want to do one of the following:

- **Postsolution Reflection:** Have students complete a reflection sentence frame (see below) *after* they have worked on the problem and solutions have been discussed.

- **Beat-the-Bell Reflection:** Schedule the Three Reads for the latter part of a lesson and have students solve the problem for homework. In this scenario, you can end the Three Reads by having students reflect on what they learned about reading and interpreting a math problem. You might also invite students to jot down a few ideas about how they might enter the problem to set up their problem-solving homework.

- **Targeted-Transition Reflection:** Prompt a quick turn-and-talk at the end of the Three Reads where students share with their partner one thing a classmate paid attention to while interpreting the problem that they might incorporate in their problem-solving plan.

However you choose to build in math practice reflection time, here are some sample MP1 reflection sentence frames:

- When interpreting a word problem, I have learned to ask myself _____.
- The next time I read a word problem, I will pay attention to _____ because _____.
- Mathematicians read word problems for _____.
- When looking for important information in a word problem, I have learned to _____.
- This is an example of a _____ type of problem because _____.

The Important Takeaway

The overarching goal of the Three Reads instructional routine is to develop students' capacity to read and interpret a math word problem. So although it is important to consider the complexity of the language and how that complexity increases the cognitive load for ELLs and students with learning disabilities, be careful not to overscaffold the supports. *All* students are learning to read mathematically. That means *all* students must struggle with finding the mathematics underneath the problem context and that mathematics can be brought to light through the three avenues of thinking. It's important to provide comprehension supports only insofar as they take away barriers to understanding the problem context. Once students understand the context, *they* can begin the work of "mathematizing" the situation, using the three avenues of thinking: finding the quantities and relationships in the context, describing the behavior of the situation, and articulating any repetition in process. Then *they* will be reading like mathematicians!

In the final chapter, we'll dig into some details and suggestions for planning your own use of any of these routines.

Making It Routine

Implementing Instructional Routines

If you are reading this chapter, we hope it is because you see the promise of the instructional routines and want to give them a try. This chapter provides a plethora of suggestions and supports for getting started. Unlike the other chapters, this one is written to allow you to skip around, picking and choosing what you need from the information provided here. We'll begin the chapter with some important overarching considerations, and then we'll dig into specific recommendations and supports.

Before You Start

We have worked extensively with teachers learning to use these routines and have coached teachers in their own classrooms to help them hone their implementation of these routines. As a result, we've learned several lessons that we feel are important to share at the outset:

- **Pick one routine and get comfortable with it before taking on another routine.** We strongly recommend picking one routine to start with, both to allow yourself time and opportunity to gain familiarity and to maximize the impact the routine can have on your students' thinking. Trying to juggle learning more than one at a time can quickly become a bit overwhelming.

- **No matter which routine you pick, plan on enacting it at least four or five times over a relatively brief time frame (two weeks or so) so that it can become "routine."** The value and the impact of these routines come from making them routine. So we encourage you to treat them not as an interesting activity to try out, but as a habitual way of doing math to develop your students' capacity to think mathematically. As with any new classroom routine you introduce, students need to experience it frequently enough to start making it habitual; these routines are no different.

- **After learning the first routine, you and your students will learn additional routines more quickly.** Each routine contains similar elements, so when you introduce a second routine, you and your students will already be familiar with the typical launch of the routine, with the think-pair-share structure that permeates each routine, and with the structure and purpose of the final reflection. Your collective learning of the second routine will happen more easily, and even more so with the third. So allow yourself the time and patience to have a learning curve as you and your students work to make sense of your first one.

Everyone has his or her own preferred way to learn how to use a new instructional tool. We expect that some of you will prefer to start by not straying too far from the examples we've provided in this book, and others will prefer to make different choices for think-ing goals, ask-yourself questions, sentence frames and starters, and student reflection prompts, and to tailor the routine specifically to the needs of your students right away. In our own work, we've often seen teachers move from the former to the latter, starting first from our suggestions for math problems, questions, and reflection prompts in the rou-tine, then to adapting those recommended pieces, and finally to choosing their own math problems and creating their own thinking goals, ask-yourself questions, sentence frames and starters, or student reflection prompts.

Getting Started

You may be feeling at this point like there are many moving parts to these routines, and a little unsure about how to begin. Here is a "quick start" guide of sorts. We'll go into more detail on much of this later in the chapter, if you're ready to do more customization, but this should be enough for your first time using one of these routines.

- **Decide on a routine.** There is no prescribed order in which to take on the instructional routines in this book. Simply pick one. Begin where you are in the content or with the routine that most interests you or with the avenue of thinking you feel makes the most sense for your students to learn first.

- **Decide on a math problem to use in the routine.** As a starting point, we recommend using the math problem that was played out in the appropriate prior chapter or choosing one from Appendices C–E. The problems we have included are tried-and-true, and many teachers and students have used them. Find one that you like and try it. In fact, try two or three of the problems we've provided.

- **Do the math**. By "do the math," we don't mean "make sure you can get the answer"; we mean preview and reflect on the mathematical thinking that you will be asking the students to do when they are, for example, creating the diagrams; connecting the representations; counting, constructing, or calculating; or reading three times. Doing the math for yourself is critical to the success of the routine because it prepares you to understand how a particular avenue of thinking arises from the problem in the routine. It may be tempting to skip this step because you already know the answer or you assume that you can do it in the moment, but we strongly recommend that you don't. You do the math to note what you are paying attention to, which ask-yourself questions you are using, and the particular actions, specific to an avenue of thinking, that you are taking. Doing the math will help you to notice when students are using the avenue of thinking and help you develop language to discuss that avenue of thinking. After you do the math, think about how you expect your students' approaches to be like or different from yours.

- **Tailor the routine to your classroom.** For each routine, you have choices to make about your thinking goal, about which ask-yourself questions to use in the routine, about which sentence frames or starters you will use, about what and how to annotate, about how to use the Four Rs in any whole-class discussions, and about what prompts to include in the final reflection in the last step of the routine. If you prefer to keep your choices simple, we recommend you look at the specific suggestions we offer for each of these things in the previous chapters and later in this chapter; the easiest way to test-drive one of these routines is just to use the suggestions found there. As you gain more familiarity with the routine, you may feel ready to tailor those suggestions more closely to your classroom, or to create your own.

Now that you've done the quick-planning version of preparing to use your chosen routine, try it out with your students!

Getting Comfortable with Your First Routine

All the vignettes in the book provide images of what it looks like once both the students and teacher have become familiar with the routine. In the vignettes, everything goes perfectly smoothly and the students know exactly what to do. But how do they get there? How exactly do you introduce a routine? What's different the first couple of times? What are the potential pitfalls? In this section, we will address questions related to the first few times you use a routine.

When should it feel familiar?

It will take between three and five enactments for you and your students to get comfortable with the routine. As with any classroom routine, both you and your students will internalize these instructional routines as they become more familiar. So we encourage you to be forgiving of yourself and your students these first couple of times, and allow yourselves time to have a learning curve before judging your own or their participation in the routine.

There are so many things to pay attention to. How do I remember all these parts?

When first introducing a routine, we recommend focusing on simply following the steps of the routine to become familiar with that flow, saving attention to other aspects, such as discourse, digging into mathematical thinking, supporting language development, and so on, for a little later in your implementation. This will help keep it more manageable for both you and your students. A routine becomes "routine" when it's a familiar set of steps that require little or no direction to move through. So focusing on the flow of the routine is an important first step to helping your students (and you!) become familiar with the parts of the routine and how they work together.

To focus on flow, think "frame, name, and keep it the same."

- **Frame the flow of the routine.** Provide a general overview of the routine to your students—a road map of your path through the routine. This also includes a quick summary of what will happen in each part of the routine as you go along. In effect, you're pausing along the way to show students where they are on their routine road map and to help them understand what will happen in that part.

- **Name the parts as you get to them**. To help build familiarity, give the different parts a label, such as "individual think time," "working with a partner," and so on, then use those labels consistently.

- **Keep it the same.** Keep the enactments of the routine consistent each time. Following digressions or skipping parts, especially in the beginning, will make it difficult for students to follow the routine. To learn the routine, students need to recognize what's the same each time and what makes it a routine as opposed to an individual classroom activity.

  If you use slides, try to use the same ones each time and simply insert the new problem. The consistency of the instructions, formatting, and cues on the slides help students to key in on what is staying the same each time. It will also help you know what's coming next! And, as we've said earlier, this consistency and additional modality is especially helpful for struggling learners. We've included a copy of one sample set of slides in Appendix B that you can work from. Whatever slides you use, we recommend keeping the formatting, icons, and language the same across enactments of the routine.

What are my students likely to do? Will they be able to do this?

One of the most challenging shifts for students to make when they first experience one of these instructional routines is focusing on their thinking. Students are well practiced in getting answers and explaining the steps they took to get their answer. The routines, on the other hand, ask students to focus on the mathematical thinking that resulted in the approaches they took to answer the question. So you can expect that, in the beginning, no matter what question you ask to prompt their thinking, many students will hear it as you asking for the answer. For example, in Connecting Representations, you might ask students, "What did you notice that was the same about the representations?" and students will answer, "The first graph goes with the second equation." In Capturing Quantities, you will prompt students to create a diagram that captures important quantities and relationships, and as you walk around the room—rather than seeing diagrams—you will notice several students calculating the answer to the problem. This doesn't mean that students cannot or will not engage in or discuss the thinking, it simply means that it's not what they are expecting to do. So to get (and keep!) the avenue of thinking front and center for students:

- Remind students that they are not answering the problem (yet)—they are identifying important quantities, or looking for a repetition in their building process, or describing what they noticed about the representation when they were making a connection. Every time you transition to a new bit of the routine, remind students to keep the focus on the thinking. The easiest way to do this is to take advantage of the math practice-focused prompts built into the routines.

- When students do give you the answer instead of describing their thinking, make sure you avoid the pitfall of turning the discussion away from the thinking.

  - Sometimes this "tug" toward talking about the answers comes from *students*. When it does, keep in mind that your goal is to develop the thinking; take it in stride and keep going. Our two preferred ways to respond are either, "OK, so that's the answer. *And* what we're wondering about is . . ." (pointing back to a sentence frame or ask-yourself question), or "That's the answer. Now tell us what you *noticed* in the problem when you first started it."

  - Other times, *you* may feel a strong tug toward discussing the answers. If you do, try to also include discussion about the thinking, because understanding the thinking process will help students make sense of and solve future problems.

- Provide the reason that you're all working together to focus on students' thinking. For example, you might say, "I'm asking you to make a diagram, instead of just solving the problem, because making a diagram will help you think about how the different quantities in the problem relate to each other. And being able to describe and represent relationships between quantities will help you be a better problem solver." Providing a rationale for what you're doing will help students see the power in developing the thinking and see that math makes sense.

I'm not used to having a thinking goal and a content goal. How do I focus on the thinking goal?

When you use one of these routines, you need to embed it in particular mathematics content. Because of the pressures we all have as teachers to cover material, there is always an urgency to move through our content, so putting the mathematical thinking in the forefront and the content in the background, even just for one lesson, may be challenging. The good news is that these routines are forgiving. You will be incorporating these routines into your practice on a regular basis, so if the thinking fades to the background once or twice, there will be other opportunities. Using the ask-yourself questions and sentence frames and starters can help you maintain a focus on the mathematical thinking goal.

How long should one of these routines take?

On average, a routine will take 30–45 minutes the first couple of times you enact it, then as it becomes more routine, it will take 20–30 minutes, though this will vary depending on your students and the problem you select.

One common pitfall is getting bogged down in a section of the routine trying to get it perfect or being too thorough. It's more important the first couple of times to keep the routine moving so that students experience the full routine than it is to make sure they all precisely describe their mathematical thinking or carry on a lengthy full-group discussion. If students are starting to lose focus or struggle staying in a partner or full-group conversation, move on. As you use the routine again and again, students will develop the thinking and discourse skills. In the beginning, it's more important that they get comfortable with the steps of the routine.

Getting Comfortable with Student and Teacher Roles in the Routine

The routines in this book place a premium on classroom discourse. This stems from our belief that knowledge is constructed socially and our commitment to language-rich learning environments, particularly in math class. This focus shapes your and your students' roles in the classroom. Figures 7.1, 7.2, and 7.3 articulate students' and teachers' roles during individual thinking time, partner work, and group work. They list pitfalls to avoid and give general recommendations.

	What It Is	What It's Not
Student Role	• *Begin* the problem at hand (e.g., identify important quantities, analyze representations, settle into a regular constructing process, articulate the problem question, etc.). • Prepare to work with a partner.	• *Complete* the problem (e.g., create the diagram, connect the representations, generalize the repetition, answer the question, etc.).
Teacher Role	• Silently observe what students are doing. • Privately remind students of the directions if they are off task.	• Interrupt student thinking to ask students questions about their thinking. • Explain how students should be thinking.

Figure 7.1

Independent Think Time

Pitfalls to Avoid

- Letting individual think time go on for too long so that students move beyond the initial thinking to completing the problem. (This think time is typically short, ten seconds to two minutes depending on the problem.)

Recommendations

- Stop individual think time as soon as you see students start to move beyond the initial thinking.

- Remind students of the purpose of the individual think time and that they will not have time to complete the problem, just to begin thinking about it so that they can work productively with a partner.

Partner Work

	What It Is	What It's Not
Student Role	• Work together at the task at hand. • Share what they paid attention to and the questions they asked themselves. • Practice how to say or write math thinking more clearly and with greater mathematical precision.	• Work on your own. • Tell your partner the answer or show them how to solve the problem.
Teacher Role	• Look/listen for evidence of the avenue of thinking. • Observe students to see how they are thinking and what they are paying attention to or asking themselves. • Select and sequence ideas to share in the full group. • Remind students of the directions if they are off task.	• Interrupt partner work to ask students questions about their thinking. • Start explaining how students should be thinking.

Figure 7.2

Pitfalls to Avoid

- Waiting for all pairs to finish talking before transitioning to the full group
- Getting stuck listening to only a few pairs

Recommendations

- Remind students of the purpose of the partner work, underscoring that they will be working together to achieve it.
- Provide sentence stems and frames to support partner discussions.
- Use ask-yourself questions to reengage stalled pairs.
- Tour the room as pairs work to get a sense of the range of thinking in the room.
- Give partners a heads up that you are going to ask them to share in the full group. This can include being specific about what part of their thinking you want them to share. It can also include prompting them to practice how they are going to say their idea, directing their attention to highlighted language or sentence frames or starters.

Full-Group Share

	What It Is	What It's Not
Student Role	• Describe how they and their partner thought about the problem. • Listen to, make sense of, build on, and critique each other's thinking. • Identify how others used the avenue of thinking. • Explain their thinking with greater degrees of math precision.	• Focus on the answer and steps taken to solve the problem. • Talk and listen only to the teacher. • Give a one-way presentation of their own work.
Teacher Role	• Facilitate student-to-student interactions. • Focus the discussion on the avenue of thinking. • Annotate, highlight, and underscore examples of the avenue of thinking. • Model academic language. • Press students to use more and more mathematically precise language.	• Demonstrate, show, and/or explain to students how to think.

Figure 7.3

Pitfalls to Avoid

- The teacher showing or explaining a student's thinking
- Losing the thinking focus and starting to teach math content
- Making claims about the validity of student thinking (versus prompting students to critique each other's thinking). For example, saying, "That's correct Ryan. Did everyone else get that rule?" instead of asking, "Does Ryan's rule accurately capture the repetition in his calculations?"
- Facilitating a full-group conversation in which only a few students engage and/or one that is between teacher and student rather than between students
- Starting to talk about a projected piece of student work without giving students time to process the work first

Recommendations

- Remind students of the purpose of the full-group share: to focus on the mathematical thinking.
- Use sentence stems and frames to focus and support full-group discussions.
- Use the Four Rs to ensure that all students have heard the idea being discussed in the full group.
- Use annotation to focus student attention on the thinking and help them connect the verbal to the visual.

Planning in Depth

As you become familiar with the flow of the routines and how your students respond, you can begin to customize the routine based on your specific learning goal, your students' needs, and the problem you chose. The following steps will help you customize and prepare to enact any of the instructional routines in this book:

1. Choose a routine.
2. Choose a problem to sit in the routine.
3. Do the math, anticipating student responses.
4. Articulate your thinking goal.
5. Craft your thinking prompts.
6. Write math practice reflection prompts.

Choose a Routine

There are two ways to connect the routines with your content: either starting from the routine and choosing appropriate content to fit it, or starting from the content you're currently teaching and matching a routine to it.

Either way, it is helpful to ask yourself, *In what kinds of problems and content is this avenue of thinking helpful?* For example, if you want to develop your students' capacity to reason quantitatively, look for places in your curriculum where students are required to identify quantities and represent and use the relationships between those quantities to develop content understanding or solve problems. This type of reasoning is nearly unavoidable in the grade 5–8 mathematics curriculum (and in mathematics in general!). Students are asked to reason quantitatively when they solve many kinds of word problems; understand that rewriting an expression in different forms in a problem context can shed light on the problem and how the quantities in it are related; and use functions to model relationships between quantities, to name just a few.

When it comes to structural thinking, a unit in which students use visual fraction models and equations to represent word problems involving division of fractions is a good fit because of the focus on interpreting different representations. An algebra unit that develops connections between proportional relationships, lines, and linear equations would also fit this avenue. A geometry unit that has students drawing, constructing, and describing geometrical figures and relationships between them would invite repeated reasoning because of the opportunity to draw or construct similarly each time, as would an operations and algebraic thinking unit in which students are writing simple expressions that record calculations with numbers.

Choose a Problem

You don't need new materials to develop avenues of thinking; you need to look at your curriculum materials with new eyes. Your text already poses math problems that require students to identify quantities and the relationships between them, to look for and leverage mathematical structure, and to generalize repetition. Many of these problems require students to read and interpret problem contexts. We have included some sample problems for each of the instructional routines in this book in Appendices C–E, and initially you may want to draw from those. Looking across the set of problems for a given instructional routine will help you develop an eye for the types of problems that work well in each routine.

Problems for Capturing Quantities (see Appendix C)

Be on the lookout for problems that have students considering quantities and relationships between them. For example, word problems that require students to use concepts related to fractions, ratio, rates, or proportional relationships often lend themselves to quantitative reasoning. Problems that focus on the use of expressions, equations, and functions may also lend themselves easily to describing quantitative relationships.

Choose problem contexts that are familiar to your students. This will support both English language learners and students with language-based learning disabilities. A recognizable context not only increases the likelihood that students will understand more of the descriptive language in the problem setting, it also allows students to leverage what they know about the context as they make sense of the mathematics.

No matter which flavor of problem-solving task you choose, we recommend omitting the question and placing only the problem stem at the center of the routine, at least the first few times students work with the routine. Doing so helps students learn to focus on quantities and relationships, because problem stems keep students' focus on identifying and reasoning about the quantities and the relationships between them rather than bypassing them to focus exclusively—and quickly!—on finding the answer. After students have identified and represented the quantities and relationships in the problem stem, they can craft questions for the situation, giving them an additional opportunity to develop quantitative reasoning.

Problems for Connecting Representations Routine *(see Appendix D)*

The generic "problem" that sits at the center of the Connecting Representations routine is matching a set of three pairs of representations, such as word problems and algebraic expressions, fraction calculations and number line models, data sets and displays of the data sets, or geometric statements and visual representations of the statements. Ideally, the representations you choose will allow students to interpret chunks of one representation and connect those chunks to pieces of the other representation type, or notice how the form of one representation was changed and then using that difference to make the connection. Although you will not necessarily find three sets of representations sitting in your text all ready to go, it is nearly impossible to find a mathematical idea in your curriculum that can be represented in only one way, and there is no lack of representations to choose from. We describe quantities, properties, and relationships in words, with numeric and algebraic expressions and equations, and by using tables, graphs, and other visuals. We use models such as number lines, bar diagrams, and area models to develop conceptual understanding and visualize operations.

The question is, how do you put together a set of representations for the problem in the routine?

- Look for opportunities where there is already a connection between multiple representations. For example, connecting combinations of tables, rules, graphs, and word problems is a staple of every algebra curriculum. Pairs of any two of those types make great fodder for the Connecting Representations routine. Sometimes multiple-choice questions will provide one representation to match to others in the choices; these problems can also provide material for creating a problem set.

- Look for a model that your curriculum materials use to develop understanding of a math concept. For example, your materials may connect rational number addition and subtraction problems to a number line diagram. Similarly, your materials may connect fraction multiplication problems to area models. You can build from these to create your own sets of representations. (See Task Set 4 in Appendix D.)

- Select representations that play to your students' learning strengths. For example, if you have strong visual-spatial processors, use at least one visual representation. Balance these representations with another representation that students may find more challenging to help them develop their "math muscles." (See Task Set 3.)

- Put together a set of representations that target a common mistake or misconception. For example, as we did in Chapter 4, you might have students connect verbal stories of a situation to time–distance graphs of the same situation to address the common misconception that a graph is a picture of the actual motion. Because a second representation type often helps students to "see" how something is behaving, pairing representations that highlight the mathematical behavior of some situation can be a useful basis for a problem.

- You can identify or create pairs of representations that develop precision in mathematical language by connecting words to visuals or words to symbolic representations. Creating a set of representations that pair words with visuals or symbols not only supports language development but can also highlight structural aspects of a visual or an algebraic expression. (See Task Set 2.)

Avoid representations that can be matched simply because of a surface feature, rather than because of the similarity in mathematical structure. For example, when students match algebraic expressions to word problems, they can easily match them according to the numbers in each representation if the numbers are different across the representations. Make sure the numbers in all three word problems and expressions are the same, so that students cannot simply rely on matching by the numbers.

Problems for Recognizing Repetition Routine *(see Appendix E)*

When choosing math problems for the Recognizing Repetition instructional routine, look for problems in which there is an opportunity to explore a "generalized process." Generalization is a big idea in the middle grades, so curriculum materials are littered with opportunities for generalizing.

- Look for patterns in which students are asked to "find a rule." In fifth grade, these rules are often numeric or word-based. By grade 6, students are beginning to use algebraic notation to represent their rules. The two problems in Chapter 5 are examples, as is Task 1 in Appendix E.

- Look for problem situations that contain a recurring process that students can act out or model with manipulatives or track on paper. The Trolls problem in Chapter 6 is an example of this type of problem, as is Task 2 in Appendix E.

- Look for word problems in which students can try several numbers, record their calculations, and be on the lookout for a set of calculations that keep repeating. The running-laps problem from Chapter 1 is an example of this type of problem, as is Task 3 in Appendix E.

- Often texts will introduce a rule, such as exponent rules in grade 8 or integer rules in grade 7, by having students complete a set of calculations and notice a pattern or notice regularity in their calculation process. These little problem sets can be adapted for the routine. Tasks 4 and 5 in Appendix E are examples of this kind of problem.

No matter what problem you choose, you will need to think about how you will have students engage in the process. Will they be counting to find a quick way to determine "the number of . . . ," calculating to find a generalized set of computations, or constructing to generalize a building process? You want your students doing a process over and over again so that they can identify and use it, then record, condense, and ultimately generalize that repetition.

Problems for Three Reads Routine

Selecting problems for the Three Reads instructional routine is a bit more straightforward, as pretty much any problem can be a Three Reads problem. The question to ask yourself is *Will my students have trouble reading and interpreting this problem?* If the answer is yes, then it's likely a good candidate. You might want to start with traditional math word problems where students must interpret the context as well as the mathematics under the surface. Once students have gained familiarity with the Three Reads process, move on to problems with no text that include visuals and data displays to interpret. We are fond of placing test-prep questions at the center of the Three Reads instructional routine because the utility of the process becomes immediately apparent to students!

The choice of task for this routine depends very much on your purpose. If the purpose is for students to learn the routine, you don't want a task with complex wording. On the other hand, if they have become familiar with the routine, it's time to tackle some more complicated word problems like the one we used in Chapter 6. This choice also depends on your class makeup; if you have a number of emerging English learners even a more simply worded task will be tricky. The bottom line is, decide based on what your purpose is for your students.

Do the Math

This first and most critical step in the planning process is to "do the math," to preview the mathematical thinking that you will be asking the students to do. To help guide your own work in "doing the math," Figure 7.4 provides specific suggestions for each instructional routine.

Instructional Routine	Doing the Math
Capturing Quantities	• Identify all the quantities and relationships in the problem, both explicit and implicit. Note which quantities have known values in the problem statement and which are unknown. • Describe each quantity and relationship in more than one way. • Create more than one version of a diagram to anticipate what students are likely to create. • Try out different ways of annotating the diagrams using size, color, line types, etc., to highlight quantities and relationships. • Identify language essential to doing and discussing the math.
Connecting Representations	• Decide which one of the six representations you will ask students to create in Part 3 of the routine. • Identify the aspects of each representation that students will have to notice to connect them. • Try out different ways of annotating the representations to highlight structural thinking to prepare for how you will do this in the moment. • Anticipate the connections students will see and the missing representation they will create. • Identify language essential to doing and discussing the math.
Recognizing Repetition	• Engage in the process of counting, calculating, or constructing in more than one way. • Note how you sensed the repetition. • Try out different ways of annotating and recording to prepare for how you will do this in the moment. • Anticipate how students will count, calculate, or construct, and what their generalizations might look like. • Identify language essential to doing and discussing the math.
Three Reads	• Read the problem three times and answer the questions: What's this problem about? What am I trying to find out? What is important information? • Anticipate student responses to each of the questions. • Decide the avenue(s) of thinking you want to highlight. • Consider the language complexity of the problem, e.g. familiarity of context, mathematically significant vocabulary, and length and complexity of sentences.

Figure 7.4

Articulate a Thinking Goal

The purpose of creating and using a thinking goal is to make clear to students—and to yourself!—what they will learn about thinking mathematically. This is different from, but complementary to, the goal you have for them that specifies the mathematical content they are learning. Consider the aspect of the avenue of thinking you would like your students to develop and then articulate a thinking goal to communicate that type of reasoning.

When articulating a thinking goal, it's helpful to ask yourself the following questions:

- What is it that I want students to learn about?
  - Quantitative reasoning, from creating diagrams that capture the important quantities and relationships in this problem?
  - Structural thinking, from connecting the representations I have chosen?
  - Repeated reasoning, from generalizing repetition they find in their counting, calculating or constructing process?
  - Interpreting this math problem?

Instructional Routine	Sample Thinking Goals
Capturing Quantities	• I can identify quantities and relationships in problem situations. • Look for quantities and relationships that are implied in problem situations. • Learn to ask yourself, *What can I count?* and *What can I measure?* to identify quantities in a problem. • I can create a diagram that shows how quantities are related. • I can use a diagram to surface hidden relationships in the problem. • I can describe relationships between quantities in multiple ways.
Connecting Representations	• Think like a mathematician: Chunk complicated algebraic expressions into pieces that you can interpret. • Effective math doers change the form of an irregular shape to make it easier to work with. • Students will be able to connect numeric expressions to visuals by considering the rules of operations. • Think like a mathematician: Learn to change the form of a numeric expression in order to calculate more quickly. • Effective math doers think about how rewriting an algebraic equation might give them insight into how a function is behaving.

Figure 7.5

- Why am I asking students to:
  - Diagram this problem stem?
  - Connect these representations?
  - Generalize this counting/calculating/constructing process?
  - Interpret this math problem?
- What quantitative/structural/repeated thinking language am I asking students to develop?

Figure 7.5 shows sample thinking goals for each avenue of thinking. These goals help maintain focus on the thinking and also provide a vehicle for building common language around the avenue of thinking. Note that we've written the goals in a variety of different formats so that you can find examples that best suit your teaching style and preferences. Note also that different goals highlight different aspects of the avenue of thinking. Each time you use the routine, you can focus on different aspects of the avenue of thinking by using different thinking goals.

Instructional Routine	Sample Thinking Goals
Recognizing Repetition	• Think like a mathematician: Learn to ask yourself, *Do I keep doing the same thing over and over again?* • Look for regularity in the way you are counting, calculating, and constructing. • Think like a mathematician: Find the process behind the results you are getting. • Effective math doers record their counting, calculating, and constructing processes so that they can identify regularities in their process. • I can look for and use repetition in my thinking to help me create a general mathematical statement.
Three Reads	• Read like a mathematician: Read the problem multiple times. • Learn to ask yourself, *What's this problem about?* • Read like a mathematician: Learn to ask yourself, *What question am I answering?* • Good math readers ask themselves, *What's the important information?* • I can identify important information in the problem. • Students will be able to state the problem question clearly and completely in more than one way.

Figure 7.5 (continued)

Craft Thinking Prompts

Once you know the problem you are using and have decided on a thinking goal, it is time to choose the mathematical thinking prompts that will keep your students clearly focused on the avenue of thinking. These thinking prompts include the ask-yourself questions and the sentence starters and frames used throughout the routine. The thinking prompts play a dual role: they keep attention on the thinking and they support language development. When choosing your prompts, ask yourself:

- Which prompts will maintain a focus on my thinking goal?
- Which prompts will support the development of our common language around the avenues of thinking?
- Which prompts will target the academic language I want my students developing?

Instructional Routine	Sample Ask-Yourself Questions
Capturing Quantities	• What can I count or measure? • What quantity or relationship does this number describe? • How do the quantities relate to each other? • How can I represent this situation so that I can see the quantities and relationships? • How can I show how much bigger/smaller (how many times bigger/smaller) one quantity is in my diagram? • What quantities or relationships do I see in the diagram? • Is there a "hidden" quantity or relationship that I can now see in the representation? • What does this (expression, variable, number, shaded region, etc.) represent in the problem context?
Connecting Representations	• What type of problem is this? • Does this remind me of another problem situation? • How is this (situation, object, process, etc.) behaving? Can I connect it to something else I know? • What are the parts (chunks) of the process? • How can I get the answer without doing all the calculations? • How can I use properties to uncover structure? • How can I change the form of this (number, expression, shape) to surface the underlying structure?

Figure 7.6

Ask-Yourself Questions

Ask-yourself questions are used throughout the routines to help students focus on the avenue of thinking during individual think time and are a tremendous resource for students. We suggest categorizing them by avenue of thinking and then posting them in your room so that both you and your students can refer to them and start to internalize them as a way to engage in a particular avenue of thinking.

When selecting an ask-yourself question, think of it as a replacement—in question form—for the kind of "pay attention to" hint you might give students to get started with a problem.

Figure 7.6 shows ask-yourself questions for each of the avenues of thinking to choose from. For any routine, select one or two ask-yourself questions you want your students to use to focus their individual work. They are stated in general terms, so you might want to edit them to be more specific to the problem you have chosen and the language you are developing.

Instructional Routine	Sample Ask-Yourself Questions
Recognizing Repetition	• Is there something in this problem context that repeats or suggests some regularity? • How can I create or use a repeated process to help me figure out what's going on in this problem? • What was my process? Was it the same every time? • Am I counting/drawing/building/calculating in the same way each time? • What about this process is repeating? • How can I describe the repetition in words/variables/etc.? • What operations can I use to model this process? • How can I use the repetition to make my rule?
Three Reads	• What's this problem about? • What am I trying to find out? • What is the important information in this problem? • What am I paying attention to? • What should I be paying attention to? • What else could I be paying attention to? • What are the important quantities and relationships? • How is this situation behaving? • Is there a process that keeps repeating?

Figure 7.6 (continued)

Sentence Frames and Sentence Starters

Sentence frames and sentence starters are used in the routines to support avenues of thinking, development of language, and discourse. When you edit or create a sentence frame, consider not only where you want students' attention (e.g., on quantities, relation-ships, aspects of a diagram, and so on) but what language you want to provide as a sup-port (i.e., the words students will read) and what language you want students to develop (i.e., the missing words in the frame or stem).

Figure 7.7 shows some of our favorite sentence frames and starters to select and use in each routine. We have omitted the Three Reads instructional routine from the table because it does not focus so much on a specific avenue of thinking as it does on interpret-ing a problem situation. If you have chosen a math problem for Three Reads that clearly highlights a particular avenue of thinking and you want to focus the third read (i.e., the important information) on that avenue of thinking, you can always choose a frame or starter from the routine that develops that avenue of thinking.

You may want to edit one of these more general frames or starters to be more problem-specific when you use it. For example, if you are having students connect algebraic expressions and visuals, instead of using "I noticed _____ in the representation so I looked for _____," use "I noticed _____ in the expression so I looked for _____ in the visual." In short order, you will feel comfortable crafting your own.

Math Reflection Prompts

The prompts that anchor the student reflection in the last part of each routine help stu-dents articulate what they have learned about an avenue of thinking. This often includes:

- something new they learned to pay attention to
- a question they learned to ask themselves
- a mathematical connection they've made
- a new mathematical understanding they now have.

The math reflection is also a place where students formalize and practice writing mathe-matical language.

Choose 2–4 math thinking reflection prompts that align well with your thinking goal to allow for some differentiation, then let students choose one of the prompts to complete. (We strongly recommend completing the prompt the way you hope your students would, and then checking to ensure that this response aligns with your thinking goal.) Providing multiple options allows students to choose a prompt that matches what they noticed or matches a connection they made. Or you could make the choice for them, choosing a prompt that best aligns with ideas that were raised during the lesson. You can also offer the same prompt worded for a variety of English language proficiency levels (e.g., "Look for _____" as well as "It is helpful to notice _____ in algebraic expressions").

	For Use Anytime	For Use During Partner Work	For Use During Full-Group Discussion
Capturing Quantities	• The number of _____ • The amount of _____ • (Quantity _A_) is (relationship to) (Quantity _B_)	• How did you represent _____? • I showed _____ by _____. • The relationship is _____ so I looked for _____. • I noticed _____ so I looked for two quantities that _____.	• They noticed _____. • A relationship that I see in their diagram is _____.
Connecting Representations	• _____ connects to _____ because _____.	• I noticed _____ in the representation so I looked for _____.	• We noticed _____ so we _____. • They noticed _____ so they _____. • We/they chunked _____. • We/they changed _____.
Recognizing Repetition	• Every time _____. • It always _____. • First _____, next _____, then _____, finally _____.	• I showed _____ by _____.	• The process that kept repeating was _____. • The repeated process we/they generalized was _____. • The repetition we/they generalized was _____.

Figure 7.7

Printing the reflection prompts on a handout is helpful for students who struggle with copying information. However, remember when doing so to leave ample space in the frames to allow for students' written responses. These can always be pasted into student notebooks at the end of class.

It can be helpful to collect and share your students' responses to the reflections for future reference. Some teachers keep a collection of students' reflections posted in the classroom, while others have students record their math thinking reflections in the same section of their notebook. The next time students use the routine, you can use their responses as helpful reminders and suggestions of how to engage in that avenue of thinking.

Figure 7.8 lists mathematical thinking prompts for each of the avenues of thinking. You can revise them to be problem-specific, as well as written at an appropriate language level for your English learners.

Reflection Prompts	Simplified Prompts
Routine: *Capturing Quantities (quantitative reasoning)*	
• When looking for quantities in a word problem, I learned to look for _____. • When looking for relationships in a word problem, I learned to look for _____. • When finding quantities/relationships in a diagram, I learned to look for _____. • When identifying quantities, I learned to ask myself _____. • When identifying relationships, I learned to ask myself _____. • When analyzing a diagram, I learned to pay attention to _____ because _____. • The secret to identifying quantities/relationships in a word problem is _____.	• When capturing quantities, I look for _____. • When capturing quantities, I ask myself _____. • When capturing quantities, next time I will _____. • When capturing quantities, I learned _____.
Routine: *Connecting Representations (structural thinking)*	
• When interpreting a visual representation like this, I learned to pay attention to _____. • The next time I interpret an algebraic expression or visual pattern like this one, I will look for _____.	• When connecting representations, I look for _____. • When connecting representations, I ask myself _____.

Figure 7.8

Reflection Prompts	Simplified Prompts
Routine: *Connecting Representations (structural thinking)* (*continued*)	
• When interpreting a representation, I learned to pay attention to _____. • When connecting representations, I learned to ask myself _____. • The next time I connect representations, I will look for _____. • Paying attention to _____in a representation is helpful because _____. • A new mathematical connection I made is _____.	• When connecting representations, next time I will _____. • When connecting representations, I learned _____.
Routine: *Recognizing Repetition (repeated reasoning)*	
• When looking for repetition in a process, I learned to pay attention to _____. • When looking for repetition, I learned to ask myself _____. • _____ helps me notice repetition because _____. • One way to identify repetition is to _____. • The key to generalizing the repetition I found is _____.	• When recognizing repetition, I look for _____. • When recognizing repetition, I ask myself _____. • When recognizing repetition, next time I will _____. • When recognizing repetition, I learned _____.
Routine: *Three Reads (interpreting math problems)*	
• When interpreting a word problem, I have learned to ask myself _____. • The next time I read a word problem, I will pay attention to _____ because _____. • Mathematicians read word problems for _____. • When looking for important information in a word problem, I have learned to _____. • This is an example of a _____ type of problem because _____.	• When using Three Reads, I ask myself _____. • When using Three Reads, I look for _____. • When using Three Reads, next time I will _____. • When using Three Reads, I learned to _____.

Figure 7.8 (continued)

Moving Beyond the Routine

In this book, we've made the case for instructional routines being powerful vehicles for developing mathematical practices in all students, with special attention to English language learners and students with learning difficulties. We've argued that enacting the routines, with fidelity, on a regular basis will result in students developing three distinct avenues of mathematical thinking. And that this results in tenacious math doers, students who can persevere in their mathematical problem solving. So if you enact these routines regularly in your classroom with fidelity, what impact can you expect to see? What will it look like if students are reasoning quantitatively, thinking structurally, reasoning through repetition, and interpreting texts? In the next sections, we'll provide some suggestions for indicators that you can use to determine if "it's working."

Reasoning Quantitatively

Students who reason quantitatively think in terms of quantities and relationships, not simply numbers and keywords. They will see the numbers in a problem statement not only as something to be operated with or on, but also as a value for a quantity or as a clue about a relationship that exists between two quantities. Likewise, they will see key-words in a problem statement not only as a calculation to perform, but also as a description of a relationship between quantities. Figure 7.9 lists some indicators that provide evidence that your students are learning to reason quantitatively.

Thinking Structurally

Students who are structural thinkers see mathematics as interconnected and sensible rather than a collection of unrelated results and procedures to know and be able to do. They use what they know about properties and rules for operating with numbers and what they know about geometric relationships to find shortcuts and connect seemingly unrelated objects. Figure 7.10 lists some indicators that provide evidence that your students are learning to think structurally.

Quantitative Reasoning "Look-Fors"	
Your students know that: • A quantity has three parts—a value, unit, and sign. • The values of some quantities are given in a problem and the value of at least one quantity is not, and it's the quantities with the "unknown" values that are typically the one(s) the problem is asking you to find. • You use the relationships between the quantities to solve the problem. • Representing quantities and the relationships between them visually can help you make sense of the problem and often see a solution path.	Your students *regularly* take the following actions: • Say "the number of _____" and "the amount of _____" when talking about quantities. • Ask themselves (and answer!) the question, *What can I count or measure?* • Ask themselves (and answer!) *How are these quantities related?* • Look for implied or "hidden" quantities in problem statements and visuals. • Create diagrams (and other visuals) that capture the quantities and relationships in a problem. • Describe quantities and relationships in more than one way.

Figure 7.9

Structural Thinking "Look-Fors"	
Your students know that: • Certain mathematics problems may behave the same way, even if they look different from each other. • Sometimes you can use what you know about a different problem to help you make sense of a new problem, because they are the same in some way (their structure). • It's OK to change the form of an expression, a shape, etc., into an equivalent form because it might help you make sense of the problem. • It's helpful to look for mathematical "chunks" in a problem to help simplify what you're looking at and to help you think about the problem.	Your students *regularly* take the following actions: • Change the form of numbers, equations, or geometric figures into equivalent forms that provide insight into the problem and/or are easier to work with. • Chunk numbers, expressions, graphs, or geometric figures into parts that are easier to make sense of or work with. • Connect mathematical representations, ideas, processes, objects. • Look for shortcuts. • Ask themselves, *How is this situation behaving?* and *Can I connect it to something else I know?*

Figure 7.10

Repeated Reasoning

Students who use repeated reasoning regularly attend to patterns in their counting, calculating, and constructing processes, not just patterns in their results. Figure 7.11 lists some indicators that provide evidence that your students are learning to use repeated reasoning.

Interpreting Math Problems

Students who successfully read and interpret math word problems will not merely circle numbers, highlight keywords, and underline the question to make sense of the context and enter the problem; they will read the problem multiple times with different purposes to interpret it. Figure 7.12 lists some indicators that provide evidence that your students are learning to interpret math problems.

Helping Students Transition Beyond the Routines

We teach skills and procedures not for the sake of doing them, but so that students can apply them to their mathematical problem solving. The reason to use these instructional routines is to develop your students' capacities to think like mathematicians so that they can apply the avenues of thinking more broadly in math learning and problem solving. So the question becomes: once developed, how do you help students bring the avenues of thinking into their everyday math doing?

Prompt the Thinking

Each routine has a variety of thinking prompts, including the ask-yourself questions and sentence frames and starters. Start to make these prompts a regular feature of your instruction:

- Pose ask-yourself questions when launching a problem.
- When students are stuck, suggest an ask-yourself question to get them unstuck.
- Add ask-yourself and other math practice-focused prompts to student worksheets.
- Use sentence frames and starters to focus and support partner and full-group discussions.
- Post, refer to, and teach students to use ask-yourself questions and sentence starters and frames as resources.

Highlight and Name the Thinking

Keep the avenues of thinking on your students' radar. When you see or hear students using an avenue of thinking, draw attention to it. Name it. Record it. Annotate it.

- Develop a common language to talk about the avenues of thinking with your students. Start with the language we use in this book!

Repeated Reasoning "Look-Fors"	
Your students know that: • Repetition in their counting, calculating, or building can be seen, heard, and felt. • They can use regularities in their process to identify a generalized statement about the mathematics. • A key to generalizing repetition is to connect an aspect of the repetition in their process to a quantity in the problem (such as the term of the series, the tower number, or one of the variables in the problem). • If there is no repetition in a problem situation, they can sometimes create repetition by trying numbers and tracking their calculation process.	Your students *regularly* take the following actions: • Pay attention to how they count, calculate, and construct. • Record their counting, calculating, and constructing processes and look for repetition in them. • Show examples of using their senses to highlight repeated reasoning; for example, they might recite repetitive steps they're taking, move manipulatives in a rhythmic way through a process, draw a diagram that shows some repeating process, physically act out a process to notice what repeats, etc.

Figure 7.11

Interpreting Math Problem "Look-Fors"	
Your students know that: • Math problems require multiple readings to make sense of them. • Understanding the context and the question are prerequisites for determining important information. • The "important information" mathematicians read for is quantities and relationships, structure, and repetition.	Your students *regularly* take the following actions: • Read a problem three times: first for context, then for question, and finally for important information. • State the question in their own words. • Identify important quantities and relationships in the problem. • Identify structural elements in the context. • Identify any repetition or regularity in the context.

Figure 7.12

- Make and display posters or a bulletin board describing each avenue of thinking. Add examples to it every time you hear one in class. Invite students to do the same.

- Leverage the Four Rs: repeat, rephrase, reword, and record students' comments in full-group discussion to highlight their thinking.

Pause and Process the Thinking

Build in time to think! Create the space and vehicles in your lessons to support student thinking.

- Build in a few moments of private think time for students to process what they read, hear, or view before asking them to answer a question, work with a partner, or discuss in the full group.

- Regularly have students share and discuss how they first got started—what they noticed that was mathematically significant, what they wondered, and so on—not just the answer they got and the steps they took to get that answer.

- Provide time and prompts to have students reflect on their thinking—what they are learning to pay attention to or ask themselves, new connections they are making, and so on.

If some of the above suggestions sound familiar, it's because they are applications of the core elements and essential strategies baked into our thinking routines. Simply put, if you make the instructional practices that sit in the routines a regular part of your teaching, students will think and reason mathematically on a regular basis in your classroom.

Our Parting Words of Encouragement

By now, we hope that you have enough of a picture of the routines to begin. As you do, we'd like to summarize several key things to keep in mind:

- **The routines are about developing mathematical thinking.** Throughout the book, we've tried to distinguish between mathematical thinking and mathematical answer finding (though the former does lead to the latter!). These routines are designed to help students become more aware of different mathematical thinking avenues and to develop their familiarity with intentionally using them. You can support this during the use of the routine by keeping the instructional focus on the thinking, rather than on "what did you get?" and "how did you do it?"

- **Do them often enough to make them routine.** Developing a habit requires repetition, so it's important to remember that these are "routines," not just "activities." These routines are intended to be used frequently enough that they become "routine" for both you and your students. As the instructional routine becomes second nature, its steps will fade into the background and the mathematical thinking and reasoning will come to the fore. Over time, your students will no longer need to closely follow the structure of the routine because the mathematical thinking will have become more habitual. It will simply become "the way we think about and talk about math."

- **Follow the flow of the routine to support all students.** In the same way that cutting short a workout at the gym will not lead to a stronger body, rushing or shortcutting a math practice instructional routine will not yield the desired result. Cutting the individual think time or partner work compromises all students' ability to engage in a meaningful math discussion, as student ideas are in a nascent stage. For special populations who need longer processing time and multiple opportunities and avenues to make sense of and communicate their ideas, these shortcuts mean the difference between engaging and disengaging in the lesson. The flow of the specific steps in the routine intentionally provides support to a wide range of learners, and the prompts and instructions have been designed to keep the focus on the development and use of a math practice.

- **Be kind to yourself and allow yourself a learning curve.** Allow yourself and your students time to really learn the routines and develop the thinking. Like any classroom routine, the first few tries take more time, are less fluid, and may even meet with some initial student resistance. You will need to remind students (and yourself!) why they are engaging in the routine. We can assure you that the routines will flow more easily and quickly as both you and your students become more accustomed to them. Many of the teachers we know who have learned to use these routines report that when they were first learning, they initially left out parts of the routines or omitted important details. The good news is that you can simply add those missing pieces back in the next time you do the routine; over time, students will learn the routine. The best time to judge the effectiveness of a routine is not in the first or second use, but in the fourth, fifth, or sixth use.

All of these routines have been used by teachers and students in ordinary classrooms that face a variety of challenges. And with practice, all of these teachers have experienced success using the routines with students who, they often tell us, would not have spoken up or participated in math class in the past. A teacher in New York City summed up his experience this way:

> You have to try it for long enough where you're not noticing how it's changing, until all of a sudden you notice that it's changed. It's one of those things that builds gradually. At first, in September, I thought OK, now we did it three times. I want them to be able to share all their thoughts and be really good with strategies, and that's definitely not what happened.
>
> I realized in November or even early December, I looked around and thought *I really like the way students are talking about the math that's happening right now.* But I would admit that it really snuck up on me, more than it happened overnight. It's not that it took the kids a long time as much as it took me a long time, like the month of September, to figure out how I could use [the routine] to get out of

it what I wanted, what I wanted kids to be getting out of [the routine], and once I was doing that, the kids caught on. Once you can be clear with the kids on how you want them to share, and what you want them to be sharing, then they become much clearer with each other and the learning and the mathematical discourse really pick up really quickly.

We have confidence that you too can have success making mathematical thinking routine in your classroom, with all your students.

Appendix A

Avenues of Thinking: A Framework for Making Sense of Several CCSS Standards for Mathematical Practice

Reason Abstractly and Quantitatively (MP2)	Look for and Make Use of Structure (MP7)	Look for and Express Regularity in Repeated Reasoning (MP8)
Attend to ... Quantities and relationships	*Attend to ...* The organization or behavior of number and space	*Attend to ...* Repetition in processes or calculations
Ask Yourself • What can I count or measure? • What quantity or relationship does this number describe? • How do the quantities relate to each other? • How much bigger/smaller (how many times bigger/smaller) is one quantity than another? • How can I represent this situation so that I can see the quantities and relationships? • How can I show how much bigger/smaller (how many times bigger/smaller) one quantity is in my diagram? • What quantities or relationships do I see in the diagram? • Is there a "hidden" quantity or relationship that I can now see in the representation? • What does this (expression, variable, number, shaded region, etc.) represent in the problem context?	*Ask Yourself* • What type of problem is this? • Does this remind me of another problem situation? • How is this (situation, object, process, etc.) behaving? Can I connect it to something else I know? • What are the parts (chunks) of the process? • How can I get the answer without doing all the calculations? • How can I use properties to uncover structure? • How can I change the form of this (number, expression, shape) to surface the underlying structure?	*Ask Yourself* • Is there something in this problem context that repeats or suggests some regularity? • How can I create or use a repeated process to help me figure out what's going on in this problem? • What was my process? Was it the same every time? • Am I counting/drawing/building/calculating in the same way each time? • What about this process is repeating? • How can I describe the repetition in words/variables, etc.? • What operations can I use to model this process? • How can I use the repetition to make my rule?
Take Action • Determine which quantities/relationships are important. • Identify quantities explicitly mentioned in the problem situation. • Identify implied quantities. • Use representations to see quantities and relationships. • De-contextualize the problem situation. • Contextualize the problem.	*Take Action* • Chunk complicated mathematical objects (expressions, shapes, etc.). • Connect representations. • Change the form of the number, expression, space, e.g., create equivalent expressions. • Recall and use properties, rules of operations, and geometric relationships.	*Take Action* • Try several numbers and observe the process. • Draw or build the next several figures in the series. • Record and track calculations. • Generalize the repetition.

Appendix B

Sample Presentation Slides

Capture Quantities

Think Like a Mathematician!

Find Quantities and Relationships in Word Problems and Diagrams.

1. Identify quantities and relationships.

2. Create diagrams.

3. Discuss diagrams.

4. Reflect on learning.

Identify Quantities and Relationships

Dan and Camille each have a Video Game Shop card. Both cards combined have a balance of $350. After Dan spent $\frac{1}{2}$ of the money on his card and Camille spent $\frac{1}{3}$ of her balance, they each had an equal amount of money left on their cards.

What can I count or measure?

Create a Diagram

1. Share how you started to represent quantities and relationships.
2. Together, create a diagram.

> How did you represent _____?

> I showed _____ by _____.

Discuss Diagrams

Where are the quantities in the diagram?

Where are the relationships in the diagram?

> The relationship is _____.
>
> So I looked for _____.

> I noticed _____. So I looked for two quantities that _____.

Reflect on Learning

- When looking for quantities in a word problem, I learned to _____.

- When analyzing a diagram, I learned to pay attention to _____ because _____.

Appendix C

Sample Tasks for the Capturing Quantities Routine

Note that problem stems are provided and one possible question to pose and answer follows in parentheses.

1. Jan had a bag of marbles. She gave half of them to James and then a third of the marbles still in the bag to Pat. She then had 6 marbles left. (How many marbles were in the bag to start with?) (TIMSS 1995)

2. An ice cream costs $3.29, including tax, and a soda costs $1.24 less, also including tax. (How much do an ice cream and a soda cost together?)

3. Together, Evan, Katie, and McKenna had $865 when they left to go shopping. Evan spent $\frac{2}{5}$ of his money. Katie spent $40. McKenna spent twice as much as Evan. They each have the same amount of money left. (How much money did each have at first?)

4. On Sunday morning, Ryan and Maeve each had the same amount of money. Sunday afternoon, they each spent some money. Ryan spent $66 buying clothes. Maeve spent $39 buying a concert ticket. Sunday night, the ratio of Ryan's money to Maeve's money was 1:4. (How much money did each have at first?)

5. A fruit salad consists of blueberries, raspberries, grapes, and cherries. The fruit salad has a total of 280 pieces of fruit. There are twice as many raspberries as blueberries, 3 times as many grapes as cherries, and 4 times as many cherries as raspberries. (How many cherries are there in the fruit salad?) (Illustrative Mathematics Grade 6)

6. You have a coupon worth $18 off the purchase of a scientific calculator. At the same time, the calculator is offered with a discount of 15%, but no further discounts may be applied. (For what tag price on the calculator do you pay the same amount for each discount?) (Illustrative Mathematics Grade 8)

Appendix D

Sample Tasks for the Connecting Representations Routine

Set One: Visual representations and numeric expressions
(adapted from original task by Eddie Blum, Boston Teacher Residency, 2014)

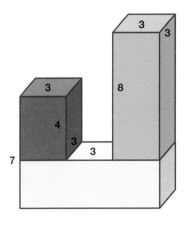

$(3 \times 9 \times 3) + (4 \times 3 \times 3) + (8 \times 3 \times 3)$

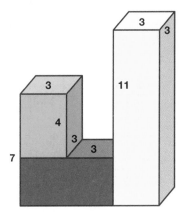

$(3 \times 3 \times 11) + (6 \times 3 \times 3) + (4 \times 3 \times 3)$

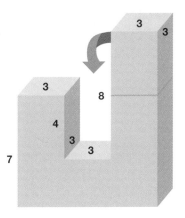

$7 \times 9 \times 3$

Set Two: Algebraic expressions and words
(adapted from original task by Meaghan Provencher, Boston Teacher Residency, 2015)

$2(x^2y)^3$ The product of x-squared and y all raised to the third power, times 2

$(2x^2y)^3$ The product of $2x$-squared and y all raised to the third power

$(2x^2)^3y$ The product of 2 and x-squared all raised to the third power, times y

Set Three: Visual representations and algebraic expressions
(inspired by visualpatterns.org, pattern #18)

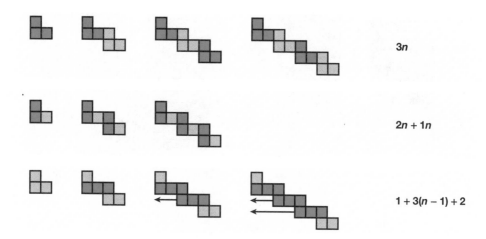

$3n$

$2n + 1n$

$1 + 3(n - 1) + 2$

Set Four: Visual models and problem contexts

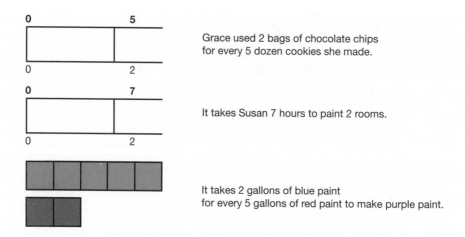

Grace used 2 bags of chocolate chips for every 5 dozen cookies she made.

It takes Susan 7 hours to paint 2 rooms.

It takes 2 gallons of blue paint for every 5 gallons of red paint to make purple paint.

Appendix E

Sample Tasks for the Recognizing Repetition Routine

1. Find a rule that you can use to find the number of dots in any figure in this pattern:

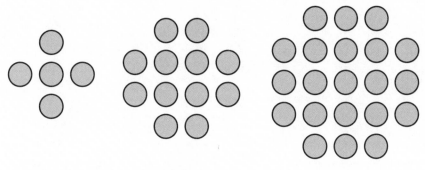

Figure 1   Figure 2   Figure 3

2. William likes to go sledding, but always struggles to climb back up the hill after sledding down, regardless of the steepness of the hill. When he climbs up the hill, he climbs up 5 feet (and it takes him precisely 30 seconds). He rests for 30 seconds, and at the end of his rest, he slides down 3 feet. At the end of the next 30 seconds, William climbs up 5 more feet, then 30 seconds later, he slides down 3 feet, and so on. The length William has to climb is 21 feet.

   a. How long will it take William to get to the top of the hill? How can you figure out the answer for any length hill?

   b. How long would it take William to climb a hill that is 30 feet long? 100 feet long? 103 feet long?

3. Lucy earns money babysitting. When she thought about the amount of money she earned over 3 weekends, she noticed that the first weekend she earned $\frac{1}{3}$ as much money as she did the second weekend. The third weekend, she earned the same amount as the first 2 weekends together. How much money did she earn each weekend if she earned $192 total?

4. Use the extended distributive property to multiply the following binomials:

$$(x + 1)(x + 1)$$

$$(x + 3)(x + 3)$$

$$(x + 6)(x + 6)$$

$$(x + 7)(x + 7)$$

$$(x + y)(x + y)$$

5. Use the definition of powers of 3, $(x)^3 = x \cdot x \cdot x$, to expand and simplify the following expressions:

$$(4 \cdot 6)^3$$

$$(3 \cdot 5)^3$$

$$(2 \cdot 5)^3$$

$$(3 \cdot 7)^3$$

$$(4 \cdot 3)^3$$

$$(x \cdot y)^3$$

References

Allsopp, D., L. Lovin, G. Green, and E. Savage-Davis. 2003. "Why Students with Special Needs Have Difficulty Learning Mathematics and What Teachers Can Do to Help." *Mathematics Teaching in the Middle School* 8 (6): 308–14.

Baxter, J., J. Woodward, J. Voorhies, and J. Wong. 2002. "We Talk About It, but Do They Get It?" *Learning Disabilities Research & Practice* 17 (3): 173–85.

Calkins, L. 1983. *Lessons from a Child.* Portsmouth, NH: Heinemann.

Chval, K. B., and Ó. Chavez. 2011. "Designing Math Lessons for English Language Learners." *Mathematics Teaching in the Middle School* 17 (5): 261–65.

Chval, K. B., and L. L. Khisty. 2009. "Bilingual Latino Students, Writing, and Mathematics: A Case Study of Successful Teaching and Learning." In *Multilingualism in Mathematics Classrooms: Global Perspectives*, edited by Richard Barwell, 128–44. Clevedon, UK: Multilingual Matters.

Daro, P. 2012. "Challenges and Opportunities for Language Learning in the Context of Common Core State Standards and Next Generation Science Standards." Conference overview paper, Stanford University, April 2012. Retrieved from http://ell.stanford .edu/sites/default/files/Conference%20Summary_0.pdf.

Driscoll, M. 1999. *Fostering Algebraic Thinking: A Guide for Teachers, Grades 6–10*. Portsmouth, NH: Heinemann.

Driscoll, M., J. Nikula, and J. DePiper. 2016. *Mathematical Thinking and Communication: Access for English Learners*. Portsmouth, NH: Heinemann.

Furner, J. M., Y. Noorchaya, and M. L. Duffy. 2005. "Teach Mathematics: Strategies to Reach All Students." *Intervention in School and Clinic* 41 (1): 16–23.

Gersten, R., S. Beckmann, B. Clarke, A. Foegen, L. Marsh, J. R. Star, and B. Witzel. 2009. *Assisting Students Struggling with Mathematics: Response to Intervention (RtI) for Elementary and Middle Schools*. Washington, DC: National Center for Education Evaluation and Regional Assistance, Institute of Education Sciences, U.S. Department of Education. Retrieved November 29, 2012, from http://ies.ed.gov/ncee/wwc/practiceguide .aspx?sid = 2.

Gersten, R., D. Chard, M. Jayanthi, S. Baker, P. Morphy, and J. Flojo. 2008. *Mathematics Instruction for Students with Learning Disabilities or Difficulty Learning Mathematics: A Synthesis of the Intervention Research*. Portsmouth, NH: RMC Research Corporation, Center on Instruction.

Illustrative Mathematics, Grade 6. https://www.illustrativemathematics.org/content-standards/tasks/1032.

Illustrative Mathematics, Grade 8, Standard 8.EE.C.7, Coupon versus Discount. https://www.illustrativemathematics.org/content-standards/EE/8/C/7/tasks/583.

Lampert, M., H. Beasley, H. Ghousseini, E. Kazemi, and M. Franke. 2010. "Using Designed Instructional Activities to Enable Novices to Manage Ambitious Mathematics Teaching." In *Instructional Explanations in the Disciplines*, edited by M. K. Stein and L. Kucan, 129–43. New York: Springer.

Lampert, M., and F. Graziani. 2009. "Instructional Activities as a Tool for Teachers' and Teacher Educators' Learning." *The Elementary School Journal* 109 (5): 491–509.

Massachusetts Comprehensive Assessment System (MCAS). 2014. Grade 6 MCAS item from 2014 MA MCAS released items. www.doe.mass.edu/mcas/2014/release/Gr6-Math.pdf.

Moschkovich, Judit. "Mathematics, the Common Core, and Language." Stanford Graduate School of Education, Understanding Language. http://ell.stanford.edu/publication/mathematics-common-core-and-language.

Ng, S. F., and K. Lee. 2009. "The Model Method: Singapore Children's Tool for Representing and Solving Algebraic Word Problems." *Journal for Research in Mathematics Education* 40 (3): 282–313.

Quinn, H., T. Cheuk, and M. Castellón. 2012. "Challenges and Opportunities for Language Learning in the Context of Common Core State Standards and Next Generation Science Standards." Stanford University, Palo Alto, CA, April. http://ell.stanford.edu/sites/default/files/Conference%20Summary_0.pdf.

Shell Center. 2015. *Mathematics Assessment Project Classroom Challenges*, T-4. http://map.mathshell.org/lessons.php?unit=8225&collection=8.

TIMSS. 1995. Released items, 1995, grade 8. http://timssandpirls.bc.edu/timss1995i/TIMSSPDF/BMItems.pdf.

Van Garderen, D. 2007. "Teaching Students with LD to Use Diagrams to Solve Mathematical Word Problems." *Journal of Learning Disabilities* 40 (6): 540–53.

Zahner, W. C. 2012. "ELLs and Group Work: It Can Be Done Well." *Mathematics Teaching in the Middle School* 18 (3): 156–64.

Mathematical Access for English Learners ... and All Students

Mathematical Thinking and Communication

Access for English Learners

INCLUDES **ONLINE** PD RESOURCES

MARK DRISCOLL
JOHANNAH NIKULA
JILL NEUMAYER DEPIPER

Heinemann
DEDICATED TO TEACHERS

Grades 4–8 • 978-0-325-07477-1 • 2016

Includes access to extensive online PD resources

Language is deeply involved in learning mathematics as students both communicate and think about mathematical ideas. Because of this, math teachers of English learners have particular challenges to overcome. *Mathematical Thinking and Communication* addresses these challenges by focusing on an essential goal: providing access to math for these students. Through a careful exploration of four instructional principles, Mark Driscoll, Johannah Nikula, and Jill Neumayer DePiper highlight powerful strategies and instructional routines for helping English learners reason more, speak more, and write more in mathematics.

> "Students, particularly English learners, are thinking when they engage in mathematics and, moreover, using language as they think."
> —*Mark Driscoll, Johannah Nikula, and Jill Neumayer DePiper*

Heinemann
DEDICATED TO TEACHERS™

Houghton Mifflin Harcourt.

www.heinemann.com

  @HeinemannPub